LT. CMDR. J. BRYAN, III, USNR
AND
PHILIP REED

First published by Duell, Sloan and Pearce, in 1945.

Copyright © J. Bryan, III.

This edition published in 2019.

TABLE OF CONTENTS

FOREWORD 7

GLOSSARY OF TECHNICAL AND SLANG TERMS IN THE TEXT
8

1 11

2 20

3 30

4 39

5 40

6 45

7 46

8 49

9 50

10 56

11 63

12 65

13	**66**
14	**67**
14	**69**
15	**71**
16	**72**
17	**74**
17	**76**
18	**77**
19	**78**
20	**79**
21	**80**
22	**81**
23	**82**
24	**83**
25	**84**
26	**85**
27	**86**
28	**88**

29	89
30	91
31	92
32	94
33	95
34	96
35	97
36	98
37	99
38	100
39	101
40	104
41	106
41	107
42	111
43	112
44	116
45	117

46	**118**
47	**121**
48	**122**
49	**123**
50	**124**
ROSTER	**125**
A NOTE TO THE READER	**134**

FOREWORD

THE concluding phase of the First Battle of the Philippines occurred on June 19, 1944. Late that afternoon, United States Navy planes from Task Force 58 attacked a Japanese fleet. They sank one carrier and four tankers, probably sank another carrier, another tanker and a destroyer, and damaged several other ships. Our losses were ninety-six planes and forty-nine men.

Vice-Admiral Marc A. Mitscher, Commander of Task Force 58, gave the order that launched the attack. The planes that delivered it were drawn from air groups based on the carriers that constituted part of his command. Air Group 16, based on his flagship, the USS Lexington, was typical of the groups participating from the larger carriers. It consisted of three squadrons: Fighting 16, equipped with F6F-3s, or Hellcats; Torpedo 16, equipped with TBM-1Cs, or Avengers; and Bombing 16, equipped with SBD-3s, or Dauntlesses.

Thirty-four of Air Group 16's planes took off that afternoon; eleven single-seater Hellcats, seven Avengers with crews of three, sixteen Dauntlesses with crews of two. The account that follows is the account of those sixty-four men. It is derived wholly from narratives by the survivors, from statements by officers and men of the Lexington's company, and from the authors' witness. No incident has been fabricated. No word or thought or action has been ascribed to anyone without his own authority.

Lieutenant Harold S. L. Wiener, USNR, was extremely helpful in supplying material for this account, and Melvin B. Dobrow, Y2c, USNR, and Forrest W. Price, Y2c, USNR, were of great assistance in preparing the typescript. The authors wish to express their gratitude.

JOSEPH BRYAN, III,
Lieutenant-Commander, USNR
PHILIP REED USS

LEXINGTON, June-July 1944
PEARL HARBOR, August 1944.

GLOSSARY OF TECHNICAL AND SLANG TERMS IN THE TEXT

acey-deucy. A favorite Navy game, a variation of backgammon.

arm-master-switch. An electrical switch which arms bombs.

artificial horizon. An instrument which shows whether a plane is laterally in level flight.

Avenger. See TBF and TBM.

barrier system. Heavy wire "fences" extending the width of the flight deck. Normally they are flush with the deck, but they can be raised to halt a landing plane whose tail-hook has failed to engage the arresting gear.

beam (as "on the port beam"). Abreast of the ship on the port side.

Betty. A twin-engine Japanese bomber. blues. A blue uniform.

Bogey. An unidentified plane.

bullhorn. A loudspeaker used on the flight deck.

can. A destroyer.

cartridge screen. A demountable canvas panel, installed to prevent empty cartridges from fouling the rear-seat controls in an SBD.

catwalks. Narrow galleries or passageways. caulked off. Asleep.

conked, (as "His engine conked"). Stopped. corpsman. A medical orderly.

Dauntless. See SBD.

ditch. To make a water landing in a land plane.

dyemarker. A packet of powder carried by all Navy pilots. Released in water, it forms a brilliant green stain, visible for great distances.

ETA. Estimated time of arrival.

F6F. The Hellcat, a fighter plane built by Grumman. fantail. The after end of the main deck.

filler pipe. A pipe from a fuel tank. flag bridge. The admiral's bridge, the first bridge above the flight deck.

flag plot. The "office" of the admiral and his staff, on the same level as the flag bridge, which encloses it on three sides.

fly contact. Flight during which the pilot can use the ground or the sky as a reference, as opposed to "instrument flight."

ground speed. Actual speed of a plane; i.e., air speed plus or minus the wind differential.

Hellcat. See F6F.

Helldiver. See SB2C.

high-side run. An aerial attack made from a greater altitude and from one side.

ID card. The identification card carried by all Naval personnel.

intercom. The intra-plane telephone. island. The whole superstructure of a carrier, rising from the starboard side of the flight deck.

jeep. An escort carrier (CVE)

jink. Short, sharp changes of a plane's course and altitude, to confuse the enemy's fire.

Judy. A Japanese dive-bomber.

Kingfisher. See OS2U.

Luftberry circle. A maneuver (named after Raoul Luftberry, its inventor) in which planes form a circle for mutual protection.

meatball. The red Rising Sun emblem on Japanese planes.

o'clock. System of indicating a direction, as "Bogeys approaching from 12 o'clock" (dead ahead) or "6 o'clock" (dead astern).

OS2U. The Kingfisher, an observation-scout seaplane built by Chance Vought.

plane captain. An enlisted man responsible for the maintenance of a plane.

probable. An enemy plane so damaged as to have less than an even chance of reaching its own territory safely.

quarter. In general, a position or direction 45° off a ship's stern.

radio shack. The ship's radio room. ramp. The bow and stern ends of the flight deck. ready room. The room in which pilots or aircrewmen await orders to take off. There are six ready rooms on an Essex-class carrier such as the Lexington.

risers. An extension of a parachute harness to the shrouds (q.v.).

sack. Bed.

SAP. A semi-armor-piercing bomb.

SB2C. The Helldiver, a bomber built by Curtiss.

SBD. The Dauntless, a dive-bomber built by Douglas. screen. The light ships (destroyers or light cruisers) stationed around the perimeter of a task group or task force.

sea anchor. A device for keeping a drifting craft headed into the wind.

shrouds. Lines or cords connecting the skirt of a parachute to the risers (q.v.).

squawk-box. Part of the ship's loudspeaker system. stinger gun. The .30-calibre gun that fires aft from the belly of an Avenger.

sure. An enemy plane which has been seen to explode or crash, or from which the pilot has been seen to jump.

tail-end Charlie. The last plane in a formation.

TBM. The Avenger, a torpedo plane built by General Motors to Grumman's design.

TBS. A high-frequency radio telephone, for Talk Between Ships.

top off. To make up any deficiency in a plane's fuel supply.

trailing edge. The after edge of a plane's wing. turtleback. The top of the fuselage, aft of the pilot's cockpit.

Val. A Japanese reconnaissance dive-bomber.

Verey pistol. A pistol which shoots flares. wingroot. Where the wing joins the fuselage. yeoman. A clerk.

zoom. To pull up a plane suddenly.

1

THESE were the last hours of the last day of the hunt. Everyone in Task Force 58 knew it. Somewhere over the western horizon its scout planes were searching the Philippines Sea, waiting for a glimpse of a fugitive Japanese fleet. On the flag bridge of the USS Lexington, Vice-Admiral Marc A. Mitscher perched in a tall steel chair, waiting for their report. Around him were his carriers, their decks packed with war planes, waiting for his signal to attack. But darkness would fall in four hours. The scout planes would be blind. And tomorrow would be too late.

A step from Mitscher's chair on the bridge was flag plot, the headquarters of his staff. They were gathered there now, filtering the radio's gabble for the words that would fire them into action. The chief of staff, Captain Arleigh Burke, was chewing the stem of a cold pipe and muttering "Damn!... Damn!...," softly, over and over. The deputy chief, Captain Truman Hedding, picked up a book, glanced at its title, Action at Sea, and tossed it aside.

The flag navigator was kidding Commander Gus Widhelm: He kept his voice low: "What'll you take for that bet of yours now?"

"Me? What bet?" Widhelm asked.

"You know what bet — that thousand-buck bet that we'd intercept the Jap fleet."

Widhelm said, "I'll sell out for fifty."

The navigator grinned. "Fifty? I wouldn't give you—"

He never finished. The radio interrupted. It said, "I see 'em!"

Widhelm jumped for the bridge. "They see 'em!" he shouted to the Admiral. "We've got 'em!"

Mitscher stepped down from his chair. "Get me the whole message."

In the radio shack two decks below, monitors stood constant guard on the channels of the fleet, typing out every word that came through their earphones. Widhelm found the transcription and read it aloud: "I see them. There's a pool of oil over there, and the nose of a Jap plane sticking up. Somebody else must have shot them down."

Flag plot's loudspeaker had faded out prematurely; this was merely a snatch of idle chatter. Widhelm had turned for the ladder to the bridge when one of the monitors pulled his sleeve and gestured toward the message his other hand was typing…

Far to the west, a scout pilot was almost at the extreme end of the sector he had been assigned to search. Suddenly he noticed strange dots and ripples in the sun's blinding path. For all his dazzled eyes could tell, they were only small clouds or their shadows. He pointed them out to his crew. Their eyes were sharper. The radioman reached for his key: "Enemy force sighted. Position—"

Widhelm spread the transcription on the chart table. While the navigator measured distances, Captain Burke began to speak into the TBS phone:

"Zebra from Camel, Zebra from Camel—"

Monitors in plotting rooms throughout the fleet decoded Burke's message as they took it down: "Task Force 58 from Commander Task Force 58 —" The enemy's position, of course, and speed followed. The message ended, "Acknowledge."

The navigator wrote a figure on a slip of paper. Widhelm whistled when he saw it. Mitscher asked, "Well, can we make it?"

For a moment, none of the staff officers answered. They were thinking of the same things: not only of the savage Japanese defense, but of the long flight home, across an empty ocean, with exhausted pilots watching the needles on their fuel gauges sink toward the "E" that meant a crash landing in the black water.

"We can make it," Widhelm said at last, "but it's going to be tight."

Mitscher gave the order firmly: "Launch 'em!"

His decision went first to his superior, Admiral Raymond Spruance, on his flagship near by: "Commander Fifth Fleet from Commander Task Force 58. Expect to launch everything we have. Probably have to recover at night."

Two minutes later, Burke started the order on its way down the echelons of command; "All task group commanders from Commander Task Force 58. Launch first deckload as soon as possible. Prepare to launch second deckload."

The task group commanders broadcast it to the captains of their carriers. The captains relayed it to their air officers. The air officers spoke to their yeomen, and presently teletypes began to stutter behind illuminated screens in the Lexington's ready rooms, in ready rooms on the Enterprise and Princeton, the Bunker Hill and Hornet, the Wasp and other carriers of the task force.

The pilots looked up from their letters and magazines and acey-deucy games. Since morning their chartboards had been filled in with data for the flight: weather information, distance and bearing of the nearest land, recognition signals and call numbers, time of sunset, proper directional approach to base. The only item missing was the one that now tripped across the screen: the enemy's position, course', and speed.

In Fighting 16's ready room, on the Lexington, Sy Seybert found that the position fell outside the perimeter of his navigating circle. He penciled a dot on the margin of the board and stared at it incredulously: "I've got to fly out to here?"

"Check, brother," they told him. "We've got to fly out to there."

Some of the pilots were already hung with their flight gear. The rest began to buckle it on: shoulder holsters, back packs, life jackets. They shook their canteens, wiped their goggles, slapped their pockets for knives, cigarettes, lighters, handkerchiefs, luck pieces. When the squawk-box rasped, "Pilots, man your planes!" they picked up their helmets and chartboards and the note-pads that clamped to their knees, and trooped up to the flight deck quietly. There was none of the usual jostling at the hatches and ladders. No one joked.

Air Group 16's planes were ready. They had been armed and tuned for hours, their engines warmed at intervals, and their fuel tanks topped off immediately afterwards. Red-helmeted firemen stood by with their extinguishers. Handlers held the lanyards of the wheel-chocks. Plane captains polished the glass canopies and repolished them. Four signal flags fluttered down from the Lexington's yardarm, and the task force began to turn. The East wind no longer blew from astern. It was on the starboard quarter, the starboard beam…

Meanwhile, the scout pilot who had spotted the enemy fleet had been dodging in and out of clouds, piecing together what he saw, and was sending in a supplementary report. Slightly south of him, another scout pilot was also reporting. Flag plot coordinated the two messages, and at 4:10 Captain Burke reached for the TBS phone again:

"All task group commanders from Commander Task Force 58. There are two, possibly three, groups of enemy ships. One group, ten to fifteen miles to the north, consists of one large carrier, two or three heavy cruisers, and eight destroyers. Southern group has two carriers, two tankers, and a destroyer, on course due west. Third, consisting of one carrier and many other ships, is sixty miles west of the center group. The primary objective is the carriers."

On the Lexington's flight control bridge, the air officer, Commander Leonard Southerland, told his assistant, Lieutenant-Commander Stephen Rice, "Start 'em up." The bull-horn magnified Rice's voice to a roar: "Start engines!"

A cartridge exploded, then another, then six, ten. The engines caught quickly and racketed to full power, with halos of pale vapor streaming from the propeller tips. The blast glued the deck crews' dungarees to their bodies, and sent small debris scampering aft. Men in the catwalks shielded their eyes and ears. The launching signal officer took his position at the starboard wing-tip of the first Hellcat in line. Clustered behind the fighters were the Avengers; behind them, the Dauntlesses, their gunners hunching down from the storm of stinging particles. The wind was moving across the starboard bow. Presently it blew straight over the ramp, and the Lexington steadied on her course.

The bull-horn roared, "Launch planes!"

A white flag with a red diamond in the center, the Fox flag, jerked up to the yardarm. A plain white flag whipped from the flight control bridge. The launching officer began to whirl a small checkered flag.

The first Hellcat was Henry Kosciusko's. As the flag whirled faster, he gunned his engine until the tail quivered and the tires on the locked wheels bulged. Then the flag dropped, pointing toward the bow, and the wingtip sliced over the launching officer's head. The time was 4:24.

Kosciusko gathered speed, leaped into the air and swerved to starboard, so that his slipstream would not batter the plane behind him. Before he had tucked up his wheels, Bill Seyfferle was skimming over the ramp. Seconds later, Whitey Whiteway was off, with Johnny Bartol on his heels.

Sy Seybert led the next division of fighters. Setting up his chartboard and collecting his gear had not left him much time for thinking about the mission, but as he waited for the flag to drop, his mouth seemed strangely dry. He patted his pocket for reassurance. They were both there — a silver dollar, the first he had ever earned, and a cheap, rusty lighter. They had gone over the side with him when the old Wasp was sunk in the Coral Sea, and he never flew without them.

Frank McPhillips followed Seybert, then Ted Wendorf and Mouse Albert, but Albert discovered a bad oil leak, and McPhillips' radio went dead almost at the same time. Both of them had to turn back.

The third division was Alex Vraciu's. Homer Brockmeyer led it down the deck, followed by Vraciu and Jim Arquette. Vraciu was the Navy's ranking ace. Eighteen miniature Rising Suns were stenciled on his plane's fuselage. The paint on six of them was still tacky; he had earned them only the day before, in eight furious minutes. Usually he was eager for a fight. When he was Butch O'Hare's wingman, they used to tell each other, "The Jap fleet is where the meat-balls grow thickest!" But something was wrong today. Vraciu felt stale and jerky. For once, he dreaded the flight in front of him. The checkered flag swept down.

Jim Arquette's Number 37 was the last of the Hellcats. Tom Bronn's Number 66 was the first of the Avengers. The launching officer held him well back of the fighters' starting line, since he would need a longer run to haul his seven-ton plane into the air with its one-ton load of bombs.

Bronn's turret-gunner, Mike Banazak, dreaded the flight as much as Vraciu. He had lost his talisman, a little plastic Scotty, and something kept telling him that he would want it before the day was over. He was turning out his pockets for the tenth time when the big plane began to roll.

Warren McLellan trundled after Bronn, then Kent Cushman. There was a wallet in Cushman's breast pocket, and an ID card in the wallet, and an English sixpence under the celluloid cover of the card — the sixpence his wife had worn in her shoe when they were married.

Clint Swanson was next. As he taxied up to the line, he glanced down at his ring. His uncle had carved it for him, and Swanson always made sure that it was straight on his finger before a take-off or a landing. His radioman, Rene LeBlanc, brushed his hand over the Sacred Heart of Jesus pin on his lapel. A home-town girl had sent it to him just before she became a nun.

Bill Linn's was the fifth Avenger. Halfway along the deck, his propeller slipped from full low pitch into medium high. It was too late to jam on the brakes; he would have drabbled off the bow. There was nothing for it but to shove the throttle forward. His plane struggled into the air and stayed up just long enough for him to jettison his bombs clear of the task force and flop down on the nearest carrier. Half his oil had leaked away in less than twenty-five minutes. A few minutes more, and his engines would have seized, frozen tight.

Linn's lumbering take-off delayed Buzzie Thomas' for fifty seconds. His gunner, Grady Stanfill, had been in the shower when the bugle blew "Flight Quarters," and his socks and drawers were clinging to his wet skin.

Thomas was another pilot who carried a memento of his wife — one of her handkerchiefs, sewn into the back of his helmet. He would no more have left it behind than Norman Sterrie would have climbed into his cockpit from the port side.

Sterrie's was the seventh and last Avenger. He had been Torpedo 16's executive officer until a week before, when he was appointed skipper to succeed Bob Isely, who had been shot down in flames over Aslito Airfield on Saipan. Sterrie was the most experienced pilot in the squadron, and one of the most daring. At the Battle of the Coral Sea he had dropped his torpedo into a Japanese carrier, then turned back and made another run to divert the fire from a squadron mate. For that, they gave him a gold star to put on the Navy Cross he had already won.

The fighters flew in four-plane sections, but the torpedo planes flew in sections of three, each section shaped like an inverted V. Sterrie led the first one with Swanson at Number 2 position, on his port wing, and Bronn at Number 3, to starboard. The second section did not follow in their air, but stayed slightly off to starboard, with Cushman leading, McLellan at Number 2, and Thomas at Number 3.

Behind them the bombers were taking off almost as fast as the fighters had. The leader was their skipper, Ralph Weymouth. As a lieutenant-commander, he was senior officer present and therefore leader of the whole attack. His squadron also flew in three-plane sections, two sections to a division, but their sections flew in line, not staggered. Jay Shields was Weymouth's Number 2, and Tom Sedell his Number 3.

Dupe Dupree led the second section, with Hoggy Glacken at Number 2 and Orv Cook at Number 3. When Dupree had pulled up his wheels and closed his flaps, he thought back to something that had happened on the deck. As he and his gunner, Dan Dowdell, ran out to their plane, they saw that it was Number 36. Dupree stopped short. "Dan," he said, "this is our big day, and we haven't got a chance!"

Dowdell knew what he meant. They had been flying together for more than a year, and Dupree had never scratched a wing-tip or punctured a tire. But twice their planes had been completely demolished. The first accident happened off Pearl Harbor. Another SBD bobbed up under them and knocked off their starboard wing, and they had to parachute into the ocean. A few months later, they were about to take off with a 1000-pound bomb. Their engine caught fire, and they barely reached shelter before the explosion. Both those planes had been regularly assigned to Rico Richter, another pilot in the squadron, and Number 36 was Richter's too.

The leader of the second division was Donald Kirkpatrick. On his forty-one previous attacks, his plane had been shot up eighteen times and shot down once. Today he saw that he had drawn Number 13. It made no difference to Kirkpatrick. He and his gunner, Dick Bentley, still exchanged their usual formula as they climbed in.

"Here we go again!" Kirkpatrick said.

"Here we go again!" said Bentley. He was the youngest man on the mission. His nineteenth birthday was only a month behind him.

The youngest pilot was Eugene Conklin, Kirkpatrick's Number 3. He had been twenty in December. He was new to the squadron, but he had already proved that he had "a feel for the stick" and that he would take his plane down in a dive until he could scrape his bomb off on the target. Weymouth had warned him against it again that afternoon.

Opposite him, on Kirkpatrick's other wing, was Don Reichel. Waiting for the flag, he remembered that this was his thirty-sixth mission and he had a sudden, terrifying conviction that it would be his last. Then the flag went down, and his apprehension dropped away with the flight deck.

Harry Harrison led the second section in Kirkpatrick's division. His regular Number 2, Pinky Adams, should have followed him off, but Adams' plane was spotted last on the deck, and Cookie Cleland, the leader of the tail-end section, took off in his place.

Harrison's Number 3 was Hank Moyers, whose gunner, Lee Van Etten, was the most superstitious man in the squadron. He always climbed up on the port wing, over the canopy, and into his cockpit from the starboard side. He always wore the same flight jacket and always stuffed it with the same litter: a pipe, one ivory die, a screwdriver, two nuts and bolts, and a pine-cone "Worry Bird."

The other gunners kidded him, but Van Etten had an answer: "O.K., so there's nothing to it, but the only time our plane ever took a hit was at Truk, and another guy was riding in my seat."

Cleland's wingmen, Willie Williams and Irish Caffey, were the rest of the tail-end section. The last man to leave the ship was Pinky Adams' gunner, Harry Kelly. As each plane rushed past, the crews in the catwalks cheered and gave it the thumbs-up sign. Kelly saw them. Thumbs up, hell! he thought. What they mean is, "So long, sucker!"

For once, Admiral Mitscher had not watched the takeoff. He and his staff were in flag plot, debating whether to launch the second strike.

The afternoon before, he had been on the flag bridge when the fighters returned from intercepting a Japanese air attack. Taxiing toward the bow, each of them had grinned up at him and had put up fingers to show how many enemy planes he had shot down — one, two, four, even six.

Mitscher had said then, "You know, I'm proud to be an American. Only the finest country on earth could produce boys like these."

Now he thought of the strike he had just launched, and the night landing ahead of it — an ordeal that might take a heavier toll than the attack itself. He thought of the second strike, and the double toll…

"No!" he said. "Hold that second strike."

He added, "I can't sacrifice any more of those boys' lives, not even for the Japanese fleet. Our Sunday punch tonight ought to do the job, and we'll get the rest in the morning. There's no telling how many planes we'll lose from this first flight. We've got to have something left to hit them with tomorrow."

Captain Burke picked up the TBS at 4:45. "Commander Fifth Fleet from Commander Task Force 58. Have launched deckload strike. Expect to retain second deckload for tomorrow morning."

When the word reached the ready rooms, the pilots scheduled for the second strike threw off their flight gear in a rising clamor of relaxed tension. In Bombing 16's ready room, someone tuned in Radio Tokyo in time to hear a news broadcast about yesterday's air battle.

"Further details of our great victory west of the Marianas," Tokyo's announcer was saying, "reveal that two American carriers have been sunk, along with a battleship of the South Dakota class, and two cruisers. Several more carriers were damaged, and at least 300 of their carrier planes were destroyed."

The pilots hooted. Not only had their fighters shot down more than 400 Japanese planes at a cost of only twenty-one of their own, but not a single ship in the task force had been sunk or even seriously damaged.

The search plane's report an hour ago had pulled the trigger on the strike now in the air, but it was yesterday's battle that had cocked the hammer.

The Japanese fleet had been prowling north for nearly a week. Navy patrol planes had seen it weigh anchor from Tawi Tawi, in the southern Philippines, and had tracked it until a few nights before, when it had been lost. In Task Force 58, Admiral Spruance and Admiral Mitscher commanded an armada powerful enough to confront almost the entire Imperial Navy. If they could find this one fleet and engage it, they might advance Japan's surrender by many months. But Spruance and Mitscher were not free agents. On June 15, American soldiers and marines had begun to invade the island of Saipan, and Task Force 58's primary mission was to assist in the capture and to cover the amphibious force. There was a mortgage on the task force's defensive power that had to be met before an offensive could be assumed. As long as the exact position of the Japanese fleet remained unknown, Spruance and Mitscher could not afford to scud off on a blind search, and thereby expose Saipan to a flank attack by carrier planes or a bombardment by surface forces.

The air battle of the 18th had voided the first of these possibilities. A sighting of the enemy fleet on the 15th had credited it with nine carriers, one of which was later sunk. The remaining eight, some large, some small, were believed to have a maximum total complement of not more than 500 planes, and at least 400 of these had just been shot down. Some of the remnant were sure to be crippled. Others would have to be saved for patrols and protection. In any case, Saipan no longer stood in danger of an air attack, and Task Force 58's radius of search could be safely extended. Accordingly, it had turned southwest-ward immediately after the battle.

By then, however, it was already beginning to suffer under a new restriction. Its destroyers were low on fuel — so low that enough was left for only a few days of highspeed pursuit. The heavy ships had ample reserves to proceed alone, but without their destroyer screen they would be open to the enemy's submarines or to a night-thrust by his surface units. Tankers were on their way out, but they still had hundreds of miles to go, and even if they had been at hand, there was no time for the laborious operation of refueling. There was no time even for the destroyers to fill their tanks from the heavy ships. With the Japanese fleeing at full speed, as presumably they were, Task Force 58 had to maintain full speed to bring them within range of its scout planes, hold the range for its strike planes, then close the range to finish off the cripples with gunfire.

It was evident by the morning of the 19th that unless the scouts found the enemy that afternoon, fuel would cost the United States Navy what might prove to be its greatest opportunity since the Battle of Midway. Now that the scouts had found them, the next step was up to the strike planes. There was nothing more that Spruance and Mitscher could do but trust them and wait and hope.

2

The strike had taken off into the steady east wind. Ralph Weymouth, leading Air Group 16's part of the massed attack, did not make the usual circles while the flight formed up. To save time and fuel, he brought his bombers around a 180° turn, holding them close to the water, and was on course at once — almost due west, into the setting sun. The torpedo planes fell in behind, at the same level, with the fighters stacked up from two to four thousand feet above, weaving to kill speed and hold their station — Vraciu, Brockmeyer and Arquette on the right; Kosciusko, Seyfferle, Whiteway, and Bartol directly overhead; and Seybert and Wendorf on the left.

Jim Seybert was uneasy. The danger and distance of the mission did not worry him so much as the fact that they had been too rushed before the take-off to coordinate their flight plans. He tried to call Weymouth, but the air was full of chatter, and he couldn't break through. He reached into his knee pocket for a cigarette. There were only two in the package. He debated whether he'd save them for after the attack, then shrugged. *I might as well smoke 'em now. I may be making a one-way trip...*

The Japanese fleet had been reported heading for a point close to the maximum combat range of the SBDs and the TBMs, so the pilots knew that the fleet was only one of the enemies lying in wait that afternoon; the other was exhaustion of their fuel. Already they had leaned their mixtures to the utmost, and the gunners had closed their canopies to cut wind resistance.

They were half an hour on their way when Weymouth heard a scout plane calling its base. The base did not answer, so he broke in. "This is Forty-one Gimlet, Forty-one Gimlet. Please broadcast all information you have. Over."

"Hello, Forty-one Gimlet! Wilco. I've got a corrected position for you, a corrected position. Ready? One-three-three degrees, three-zero minutes, East. One-five degrees, three-zero minutes, North. Course two-seven-zero. Speed one-five. That's the main body. About fifteen or twenty miles southeast of 'em is a tanker force — five tankers with half a dozen cans. Got it?"

"Thanks," Weymouth said. "Good work! Out!"

The new position was 70 miles farther than before. Weymouth signaled his wingmen, Shields and Sedell, waving his hand along the line of flight: "What is your compass reading?"

Each of them flicked his fingers. Their reading agreed with Weymouth's. He nodded, and bent over his chart-board, balancing the delicate equations of heading, wind drift, indicated speed, and movement of the enemy. His original navigation had had to be accurate within limits that were narrow enough. Now the limits had shrunk until they could squeeze a man to death.

Back in the last section, Willie Williams suddenly smelled gasoline. He looked down. Thin ripples were streaming across the outside of the approach door, a glass panel in the floor of the cockpit. Williams flew on. After ten minutes, the flow stopped. Five minutes later, he smelled gas again; the flow was heavier than before.

He called Cookie Cleland, his section leader: "Cookie from Willie. Cookie from Willie. I'm using excessive gas. My primer seems to be stuck open. I don't think I'll have enough to make the trip and get back. Over."

Cleland did not hear him. Williams called again. This time Dupree answered: "Willie from Dupe. Return to base."

As Williams curved away from the formation, his gunner, Hank Collins, asked what was the matter. Williams told him. Other gunners had happened to be flying in Collins' seat at Palau and Kwajalein, when the plane was attacked by Japanese fighters, and Collins had grumbled about his bad luck ever since. Now he said disgustedly, "Don't look like I'll ever see anything." He didn't speak again all the way home.

Meanwhile, on the basis of the search plane's report, Weymouth had altered his course from 279° to 284° and had started to climb — gently, nursing fuel. Cleland had been waiting for that move. He was the squadron's "eager beaver," always impatient until they reached bombing altitude. Before the take-off, he told his gunner, Bill Hisler, "It's our last chance to show 'em what a real dive-bomber can do. This is the job the SBD was made for — fleet action. Watch our smoke!"

Now there was something else to watch: the fuel gauge. Cleland was flying one of the squadron's oldest planes (Number 39). Its carburetor had always been greedy; today it was draining the tanks worse than ever before. Cleland didn't tell Hisler — no use alarming him. And he didn't tell Weymouth, who would certainly order him back. He looked at the gauge and hummed, "As I was sit-tin' in O'Reilly's bar—" and looked at the gauge again.

Don Reichel was watching his gauge, too. On the flight deck, he had dreaded attacking the Japanese fleet, but as the minutes passed — an hour, an hour and a half — he searched for it behind every cloud, hoping to find it before too much of his fuel had trickled away.

The clouds were deceptive in the glare of the setting sun. Twice Dowdell called Dupe Dupree to report ships ahead; he even catalogued them — so many carriers, so many battleships, so many cruisers and destroyers — but both times they turned into small clouds, low on the water. A fighter reported bogies at 2 o'clock but Weymouth recognized them as friendly. After that, the radio was silent until a voice exclaimed, "Look at this oil slick!" It was a pilot from one of the air groups which had taken off a few minutes ahead of theirs.

A second voice answered, "Haven't got time to look around! We've got to attack immediately if we're going to get back home."

Presently a third voice asked, "Is this the force to attack? My gas is half gone!"

Weymouth guessed that they had sighted the tanker force. He was sorry for those planes — half their gas already gone, the attack still to be made, and then the long flight home into a 14-knot wind. He was sorry for them, but proud at the same time: Those guys know what the score is. A lot of 'em know they are going into the drink tonight, but they're still going to make that attack!

Then he saw the oil slick himself — a bronze strip laid across the ocean. It wasn't the sort of ragged patch left by a sunken ship; it was a trail. Evidently the enemy warships had been refueling there when something alarmed them, and they had torn loose while the hoses still gushed. The tankers had left this trail, but it would lead Weymouth to the warships. He altered his course to 300°.

In a few minutes, a fighter pilot reported, "Ships ahead!" Weymouth glanced at his clock: 6:23. At 6:35, Dupree called, "Ships there — about twenty miles on the port beam." They were the tankers, but to George Glacken they looked like carriers. He couldn't understand why Weymouth kept boring straight ahead.

Weymouth had identified them correctly. They made a beautiful target, and he was tempted to hit them, but he remembered what had happened at the Battle of Santa Cruz, where all but a few planes were sucked into attacking the battleships out front, and there weren't enough left for the carriers. Today their intelligence officer had emphasized it: "Your primary objective is the carriers."

He pressed on. In front of him loomed a huge, anvil-topped cumulus cloud. At 6:45 he altered course to 310° to pass under its overhang. Presently an awed voice came over the air: "Looks like we found the whole God damn Jap navy!"

Far more ships were there now than the scout pilots had seen. They were in three groups. The main group, ten miles ahead, consisted of two Hayataka-class carriers, one light carrier, two Kongo-class battleships, two to four heavy cruisers of the Tone and Mogami classes, and four to six light cruisers and destroyers. The second group, twelve miles to the North, consisted of a Shokaku-class carrier, three to four heavy cruisers, and five or six destroyers. The third group was thirty miles west, too far to be identified or even counted.

Lee Van Etten, Hank Moyers' gunner, said aloud, "Wow!"

Irish Caffey's gunner, Dale Estrada, thought, Those Kongos are twice as big as they looked in recognition class, and that Shokaku — that's as big a ship as I ever want to see!

Weymouth had seen a Japanese carrier only once before, at the Battle of the Eastern Solomons. Shields and Sedell had never seen one. They caught his eye and held up their thumbs, grinning.

The northern group was already under attack. Dupe Dupree saw several bombs hit the Shokaku and leave it smoking. Six TBFs from the Enterprise and Hornet air groups were making runs on the heavy cruisers. Hank Moyers thought, They can't get through that fire. It's impossible!

Weymouth held his course. As they drew near the main group, Norm Sterrie, leading the TBMs, heard someone say, "No enemy planes in the air over the target!"

At that instant, eight Zekes (Zeros) dove from the cumulus cloud.

One whipped behind a TBM and opened fire. Sterrie saw the tracers flash past. A moment later his gunner, Jack Webb, called, "One man has bailed out. I—" He broke off.

"Who was it?" Sterne asked frantically. "Which plane?"

Webb had no time to answer. The Zeke was swerving into his sights. He gave it two bursts, and it fell away, smoking. Thomas' gunner, Stanfill, smoked another. Cushman's gunner, Phil Layne, smoked a third. Mike Banazak and Gene Linson, Tom Bronn's crewmen, drove four Zekes from their tail. Presently Frank Frede, Cushman's radioman, reported quietly, "Mr. McLellan's plane is on fire, sir, and they're bailing out."

McLellan was Cushman's Number 2. When the Wasp was torpedoed, Cushman had nearly drowned after only three and a half hours in the water, and he knew it would be longer than that before rescue planes could come after McLellan's crew. They didn't have a chance, especially with a tail wind blowing their chutes toward the enemy ships. He wrenched his mind away from them. Where are our fighters?

Buzzie Thomas, on Cushman's opposite wing, was abreast of the burning plane. Three men tumbled out, but he saw only one chute open. He swallowed hard to keep from vomiting. Where the hell are our fighters?

The fighters were gone. When the bombers and torpedo planes swept under the cumulus cloud, the fighters were flying high in four groups. Portside cover was Seybert and Wendorf, at 13,500 feet, about 1000 feet out from the formation and 1500 feet above. Top cover, dead overhead, was Kosciusko and Seyfferle, at 17,000 feet, with White-way and Bartol at medium cover, 2000 feet below. Starboardside cover, on a level with portside, was Vraciu, Brockmeyer and Arquette.

Just as they cleared the cloud, Seybert and Wendorf heard "Tallyho! Bogies at 7 o'clock!" Both spun to the left, but all they saw' was two Zekes, about four miles away, ducking into the same cloud. There was no chance of catching up, so they cruised in a figure-8, looking for other Zekes, then turned back to take station again. Weymouth's planes had vanished. They had been heading toward the northern formation when Seybert broke off after the bogies, so he assumed that this was still their target. A column of fire from the Shokaku carrier convinced him that he was correct. He and Wendorf circled, but no planes appeared.

Kosciusko heard the same "Tallyho!", followed by "Many Zekes above!"

He took Seyfferle up in a steep climb, but all they found was thirty other F6Fs, from other air groups. Together they headed out on their old course. Whiteway and Bartol joined them, and Arquette came over alone. None of them could understand what had become of their bombers and torpedo planes, or where the Zekes had gone.

Vraciu knew. The Zekes had sneaked in on his side, from below. He never saw them until he and Brockmeyer were surrounded — four Zekes to the left, two ahead, two to their right. One of the four on the left had already set McLellan's plane on fire. As another whirled around on Brockmeyer's tail, Vraciu signaled him to scissor and turned toward him.

Brockmeyer should have cut in and down, to draw the Zekes across Vraciu's sights. Instead, he turned levelly, and Vraciu had to bob his plane up and down again to bring his guns to bear. He fired two bursts, and the Zeke exploded, but it was too late; Brockmeyer was spiraling downward, trailing a thickening plume of smoke. Vraciu dove after him, to mark his place in the water if he bailed out, but had to pull up to dodge two Zekes behind him. He snap-rolled and caught a third Zeke head-on. It smoked, turned on its back and plunged away, but he did not see it crash in. By then he was alone. Even the Zekes had left.

After their one slash, they had sprinted to catch the bombers up ahead. Most of the bombers still had their cockpits closed, saving fuel, and the first that Weymouth knew of the stern attack was when his gunner, Bill Mc-Elhiney, called in, "I don't like the looks of those planes back there. Can I break out my guns?"

By the time Weymouth had told him, "Hell, yes!", McElhiney was already firing.

Don Reichel heard his gunner firing before he saw the Japs' tracers. He steadied his plane at once. He knew that Jack Landaker was a crack shot — he'd knocked down a Zeke at Kwajalein — and he wanted to give him a firm platform. Three 7.7s ripped through Cleland's rudder. Van Etten's cockpit was open — he was taking pictures of the ships below — but his guns were still strapped in. Something sparkled near him: it was a gush of tracers. Just as he spun around, a cream-colored Zeke darted by, three feet from his tail.

Van Etten threw the camera into the bilges and began to break out his guns. His fingers felt like bananas. Another Zeke was hanging above him. It plunged as he jerked the guns free. He could see his tracers skipping off its nose.

Three other Zekes made simultaneous high-side runs on Conklin's plane. Jim Sample, his gunner, had seen them hit the TBMs and was ready for them. He pumped bullets through one's cowling and stood up to give it a second burst as it dove under his starboard wing. Just then another shot up from below. Bentley and Landaker swung onto it and knocked down one of its wheels. Four Zekes were lining up on the two sections behind them. Harry Kelly threw a burst at the first one and turned it away. The second pressed close enough to put three bullets into the right main tank. The other two did not close.

Pinky Adams told Kelly, "Wait till they get in range!"

Kelly shouted back, "Wait, hell! I'm not trying to shoot one down! I'm trying to scare 'em off!"

It was their fleet's anti-aircraft fire that scared off the Jap fighters. In the dusk below, the ships seemed to be ablaze, so incessantly did the gun-muzzles flash and twinkle. And in the sunlight above, the bursts formed a solid roof. To Dupe Dupree, they looked like a brick wall. Irish Caffey knew it would be a miracle if he got through it alive. Thermite and phosphorus shells flung out streamers that could have covered a destroyer. The heavy cruisers were firing their main batteries; white-hot particles erupted from their shells as if from a volcano.

The volume was terrifying — worse than anything the Americans had ever met; but the colors were more terrifying than anything they had ever imagined: green, yellow, and black; blue, white, pink, and purple. Don Reichel, who was a commercial artist before he enlisted, suddenly woke from a day-dream. He had been watching bursts of a reddish-purple so brilliant and beautiful that he wanted to fly through them forever, orbiting, and painting.

The planes bucked under the concussions, but none went down. Weymouth pressed on. He had his target now: the southern Hayataka. He tried to tell Sterrie, but Sterrie couldn't receive him. It made no difference; they had led their squadrons on so many attacks, each could almost read the other's mind. Weymouth started the slow turn to port that would bring him in from the west. As the turn tightened toward the pushover-point, Sterrie held his torpedo planes wide, to clear the bombers' plunge.

Weymouth gave the right-crossover signal — right hand up, fist clenched — and waggled his wings for "execute." Shields, his Number 2, crossed above him and fell in behind Sedell. Section leaders repeated the signal down the line. Weymouth took a last look below. Both carriers had been heading north. Now they both turned west, and a westerly course would cancel the easterly wind. He thought, It's a bomber's dream! He pushed over in his dive. The time was 7:04, two hours and twenty-eight minutes after the last plane had taken off from the Lexington.

When the Zekes attacked them, the SBDs dipped from 12,000 feet to 10,500, in order to pick up evasive speed. Nine thousand feet spun off Weymouth's altimeter before he dropped his bomb, another thousand before he broke his dive. It had begun in sunlight and it ended in twilight. He plunged so low that he didn't dare close his flaps, for fear of crashing into the ocean. All the way down a rhythm was drumming in his head:

Gotta get a hit!... Gotta get a hit!... Gotta get a hit!, and he held his sights on the target until a hit was certain. Mc-Elhiney saw it: a spout of black smoke from the deck, close beside the superstructure.

Weymouth saw something more important: the carrier had reversed its rudder. If it had held around to port, the bombers' guess at its amount of turn would have complicated their aim. But a heavy ship can't spin on its heel. It would be thirty seconds, perhaps more, before the reversed rudder could bite. For those thirty seconds the carrier was committed to a straight course. The "bombers' dream" might last for the torpedo planes as well.

Behind Weymouth, Sedell had dropped. As he broke his dive, Shields shot past him. Dupree was fourth in line. The interval between planes was so short that when he pushed his release-button, the bombs from the three planes in front of him had not yet landed. His speed carried him past the first section, and out in front. Dowdell told him, "Sorry, but I couldn't see whether we hit."

It was impossible to tell which of the next half-dozen bombs was whose. Orv Cook dropped, then Kirkpatrick. He was mad when he pushed over. Just before they turned to the attack, he had heard someone say, "Let's get some hits on this carrier, and maybe they'll let us go back to the States!"

Kirkpatrick knew it was nobody from Air Group 16. What an idea for those burns, and what a time to get it! His plane, Number 13, was as old as Cleland's 39. It had no windshield heater, so the glass fogged up at the bottom of the dive, and when it cleared, Kirkpatrick found himself flying straight toward one of the battleships.

Conklin's plunge at 250 knots turned into a sickening corkscrew, and Sample was sure that Conklin had been hit, maybe killed. No use calling the kid. No time to put in my own stick. Christ, I couldn't pull out of this spin! We're going to crash! Christ have mercy! God have mercy!... Then the spin slowed. Conklin brought his sights on the target and bored on down until the last split second. He did not look to see if his bomb hit. Neither did Sample.

Most gunners face aft in a dive, but Landaker sat sideways, so that he could watch Reichel's cockpit. If he saw it splinter before they were below 6000 feet, he might have time to rip out the cartridge screen and bring the plane under control with his own stick. Dives usually scared Landaker. This one didn't. He was too absorbed in the pink and purple bursts of anti-aircraft. He told himself calmly, We'll never pull out — never, and sat back to wait for the crash.

Harrison thought, If you get through this — you won't, but if you do — you're going to be the best little boy in the world!

He pushed over. Almost at once a thermite shell burst below him, spraying its white-hot particles. Involuntarily he shrank down in his seat. Yaah, you're yellow! Could be. But I'd do the same if there were eighteen inches of steel in front of me. So much smoke hung over the carrier, he could see only its outline. Three splashes were close aboard. He felt a surge of pride in Bombing 16: Eight bombs, and only three misses! He dropped his own bomb and pulled on the stick.

Presently he called his gunner, Ray Barrett: "How'd we do?"

"Near miss," Barrett said. "About forty feet off the starboard quarter."

Harrison's disappointment lasted only an instant. "Never mind. Those five before us made a lot of those bastards jump over the side, and I bet I got some of 'em!"

Barrett added, "I thought I saw her stern lift up, so we must've damaged her propellers."

Pinky Adams followed Harrison. His bomb was a dead-center bull's-eye. Kelly reported, "Directly amidships."

As Hank Moyers pushed over, he saw a torpedo hit the carrier to the north; there was a huge explosion, and the ship listed to starboard. He half-rolled and dropped. Van Etten reported that the plane behind them had scored a hit just aft of amidships. Planes were behind them, but they were diving on another target. The hit was Moyers'.

Hoggy Glacken led the other planes down. He had dived fifth, between Dupree and Cook; but when he pushed over, the planes ahead of him were stacked up in such a way that he couldn't see the target. He skidded around for a better view and found it was directly under him, which meant a difficult dive and a probable miss.

Suddenly he saw the sister ship, to the north. He brought his sights on, but just as he released, the carrier made a sharp turn, and his bomb fell thirty feet off the stern.

Cleland followed Glacken. By now the anti-aircraft had the range and deflection cold. A 20-millimeter shell hit his right tank. A 40-millimeter hit his starboard wing, ripping a two-foot hole. Another 40 tore out the floor of the after cockpit. Hisler screamed, "Jesus! I've got the Purple Heart and no left leg!" He wasn't hurt. The hit had only made his leg numb. Cleland kicked the plane back on line and dropped his bomb ten feet forward of the stern.

Irish Caffey's was the last of the SBDs, the third to dive on Glacken's carrier. All the way down, shell fragments rattled off the skin of his plane. Estrada saw smoke burst from aft of the superstructure, but he couldn't be sure it was from their bomb.

Ten of the SBDs had dropped 1000-pound semi-armor-piercing bombs. The other four had dropped 1000-pound general-purpose bombs. At least seven bombs hit one carrier, and at least one hit the other.

Each of the TBMs carried four 500-pound SAPs, set to release in train. Norm Sterrie's target was the same as Weymouth's, and as soon as the SBDs were clear, Sterrie pushed over. The TBMs started from 9500 feet, a thousand feet below the SBDs. At 7000 feet, Sterrie opened his bomb-bay doors. At 3000, he pushed his trigger. He saw one of his bombs hit and maybe another. Clint Swanson was on his tail, then Tom Bronn. Bronn laid all four of his bombs along the carrier's deck.

Cushman brought his eight-ton plane down at 320 knots, which is 365 miles an hour. The dive was so much faster than the plane had been built to withstand, the starboard door of the bomb-bay crumpled inward, and the two bombs racked on that side skipped off it when they fell. Cushman jerked the stick as soon as he released, then shoved it forward again.

Frede called in alarm, "Are you wounded, Mr. Cushman? Are you wounded?"

Cushman yelled back, "No! Hold tight!" and started jinking. Presently Frede reported, "Two hits for us, two near misses!"

Buzzie Thomas wound up the attack. When he pushed over, the smoke from the AA made such a complete overcast that he lost sight of Cushman just ahead of him. Every gun in the fleet seemed focused on his plane. A sudden roaring made him glance over his shoulder. The speed of his dive had ripped out the thick plexiglass canopy on the center cockpit. He wasn't wearing goggles, and dirt particles began to sting his face, but he laid two of his bombs just forward of the fantail.

The Hayataka had taken seven or more 1000-pounders from the SBDs and nine 500-pounders from the TBMs. Carriers are thin-skinned. Few of them can survive nearly seven tons of bombs.

3

After a bombing attack, it is standard doctrine for planes to rendezvous on their homeward course. As soon as Weymouth pulled out of his dive, he saw that he had two choices. If he took the direct course to the rendezvous, he would bring his formation under the fire of at least two destroyers and two cruisers. If he took a roundabout course, he would spend extra gallons that might mean the difference between getting his planes home and having their engines die. He chose the direct course and the enemy's guns.

Almost at once he regretted the choice. Shells of every calibre screamed toward them and burst around them, from 20 millimetre to the cruisers' 8-inch: tracers, shrapnel, solid shot, and the thermite shells that eat up metal like a fiery cancer. Weymouth tried to make Shields and Sedell break off to a safer route, but they stayed glued to his wingtips. He was pleased, and proud of them: They're the best damn wingmen in the world!

From Weymouth's rear seat, McElhiney sprayed tracers over the deck of the nearer destroyer until one of the cruisers opened up with 8-inch incendiaries, and red-hot particles groped for his cockpit. He huddled behind his armor-plate, shuddering and praying. The other cruiser was firing its main battery into the water, hoping to knock down a plane with the spouts. Tom Sedell took his eyes from them for an instant and glanced upward. Eight Zekes in right echelon were peeling off from 2000 feet...

Dupree had pulled out to the southeast, at a speed that had shot him in front of Weymouth's section. He assumed that they would follow him, but Dowdell reported, "They're heading East."

He made a three-quarter circle to the right, to avoid a heavy cruiser on his left, but when he started to overtake Weymouth, he saw that he would fly into a solid wall of fire, and kept on around his circle. He had just passed the heavy cruiser again when a Zeke drove in toward his starboard wing. Dupree turned to meet him and pushed the trigger. His guns were jammed. He charged them and pushed the trigger again. They were still jammed. The Zeke flashed over his head without firing a shot. Dupree swung back to the east and joined up on two TBMs.

They were Sterrie's and Swanson's. After the pull-out, Sterrie had slowed down to let the rest of his squadron catch up, but when he looked around, only Swanson was there. The rest had gone off after Weymouth. TBMs have a slightly longer range than SBDs, so Sterrie could cut across a corner of the Japanese screen instead of bucking straight through. He and Swanson, jinking at fifty feet above the water, headed between two destroyers.

Past the destroyers, a cruiser opened fire. Webb, in Sterrie's turret, had been praying ever since the pushover, but the spectacle of the cruiser's shells choked the phrases in his throat. He felt grateful to the four Zekes that were diving toward him; they were a diversion. The first one attacked from dead astern. Webb put forty rounds into its belly as it peeled away and saw it crash and burn on the water. He smoked another one. As each Zeke made its run, he called the bearing to Sterrie: "Six o'clock, level!" and "Eight o'clock, high!"

Sterrie had his chartboard on his lap, trying to check his navigation. Howard Klingbeil, at the stinger gun, added his voice: "I'm out of ammunition, sir!"

Sterrie said, "Look, boys: we've got to get home. Cut out the chatter, and shoot as best you can." Just then he saw more Zekes ahead. Webb and Klingbeil heard his anguished "O Lord!"

The two destroyers had warmed up on Sterrie and Swanson. When Tom Bronn came through, he thought, Those cans have really got the word! Their bursts crept in from forty yards to thirty, twenty-five, twenty. The next one smashed into the bomb-bay.

Linson, the radioman, wailed, "Mother told me there'd be hard days, but she didn't tell me how hard!" and a moment later, "Brooklyn was never like this!"

A mile or two northeast of the southern carrier lay one of the Kongos, the battleship that Kirkpatrick found himself heading for when his windshield cleared. He kicked hard right and shot past a destroyer, which trained on him but did not fire. He kicked right again, to avoid a Tone-class cruiser, then left, toward the east. A mile ahead he saw two TBMs and an SBD — Sterrie, Swanson, and Dupree — under fire from another cruiser. Part of its fire shifted to Kirkpatrick. It puzzled him: It looks like a barrel of red-hot water! What kind of stuff is that? As soon as he saw a muzzle-flash, he ducked in and down. Between shots, he worked out and up.

Conklin pulled out at 500 feet, leveled off, then dove again until he was skimming the waves. From a thousand yards to port, the Kongo opened on him with its secondary battery. Sample swung his twin .30s toward it and fired three bursts.

"I may not have done any damage," he called, "but I'm strafing everything I see!"

The Kongo trained out its forward 14-inch turret and fired. Two waterspouts towered up, one of them twenty yards off their wing.

"You may not have done any damage," Conklin called back, "but you sure made them mad!"

He shoved his throttle forward, caught Orv Cook, and the pair of them pushed on to overtake Weymouth's section.

Cook's gunner, Pop LeMieux, was 43 — the oldest man in the air group. As soon as Cook pulled out of his dive, Le Mieux stood up to strafe one of the destroyers. Just off his port wing, a 5-inch shell burst with a bright blue flash, and a fragment ripped through his cockpit, smashing the meter of the oxygen bottle.

Cook felt the shock and called him. "You all right?"

LeMieux answered, "Hell, yes, I'm all right! How about you?" He gave the destroyer another burst.

Cook and Conklin had hardly slid into place behind Weymouth's section when a heavy cruiser, two light cruisers, and two destroyers fired on them. Two shells burst close astern, and Sample picked up his microphone to warn Conklin to jink away. Just then a third shell burst, still closer. Sample's voice came out in a squeaking "Oh!"

A fragment of the third shell punctured Conklin's canopy and rapped against his helmet. He rubbed his fingers over his head. *Wonder if I'm dead and don't know it? Nuts! It couldn't be as easy as that!*

He told Sample, "I'm hit but I don't think I'm hurt."

Sample said, "Let me know if you feel bad, and I'll put my stick in." He was worried: *A lot of times fellows get injuries like that and don't realize how serious it is. The kid might pass out and we'd spin into the drink before I could do anything about it...*

Conklin was also worried. The third shell had been so close, he was sure the fourth would get them. He split off from the others and started jinking, hard.

Harrison pulled out on Kirkpatrick's and Conklin's course. Like Kirkpatrick's, his windshield was fogged, and it cleared just in time to show that he, too, was driving straight into the Kongo. He thought, *Look at that big bastard! — She's belching fire like a wounded locomotive!* He jerked back the stick and kicked left rudder so violently that Barrett, his gunner, called, "You OK?"

"Sure, but there's this damn big battleship up here firing away at us!"

Barrett strafed it, then swung onto the small carrier. It had no superstructure and sat so low in the water that Harrison thought of the old Monitor and Merrimac — whichever the flat one was. He flew a switchback course around her and turned southwest toward the rendezvous.

Presently Reichel joined up on him. He had pulled out alone, between two destroyers which turned as he approached so that they could give him broadsides all the way. They had bracketed him with waterspouts in front and bursts behind that made the tail of his plane buck and shudder. He and Landaker could hardly believe that some of the spouts reached up to their altitude, between two and three hundred feet. After the join-up, Zekes made two futile passes at Harrison and one at Reichel, then left them alone.

Moyers' half-roll in his dive had made him pull out to the west. When he saw the "27" on his compass, he thought, Hey, I'm heading for Tokyo all by myself! He cut back to the east, past a Tone cruiser which trailed him with pink, red and white bursts. Moyers could hear them crack in his ears, and the whole plane shook.

Two planes swerved up behind him. Van Etten thought they were SBDs until one of them loomed suddenly larger and started firing. You sure aren't expecting to join up on us, are you, brother! He had loosed one burst when his guns jammed, and his stomach squeezed sourness into his mouth. The plane was black, he saw, smooth-looking, like some millionaire's racing job. You're probably a brass-hat, looking for cold chicken to tag, huh? But the black plane pulled wide. The second one closed until the cruiser's fire became even heavier, then it fell away. Van Etten wiped his mouth with the back of his hand.

Hoggy Glacken had led Cleland and Caffey down on the carrier to the north. When he pulled out, the antiaircraft fire seemed thick enough to slide down on. A black Val made a pass at him, but his gunner, Leo Boulanger, turned it off with two bursts. Glacken spotted Weymouth's section and began to pick his way toward it. Talk about running the gantlet—! Every time he thought he was through the fire, he saw more ships and guns and shells ahead. The gantlet stretched for seven miles.

Cleland pulled out in perfect position to nail the Val that had shot at Glacken, but the two-foot hole in his right wing kept dragging his guns off line. Hisler felt the drag and remembered the three hits they had taken in their dive. He called Cleland: "OK?"

"OK. Are you hurt?"

"Don't know for sure," Hisler said. "I feel kind of numb... Say, I can look straight down and see the water!"

A Zeke flashed up, and he gave it two bursts. It fell away with one of its wheels trailing and plunged in near a cruiser.

"Two of 'em!" said Hisler. He had shot down a Betty at Mille.

Dala Estrada had kept his guns hooded through the dive. After he saw McLellan's plane in flames, and the AA, he never expected to live to use them. It'll take a miracle to get me through this — that's what: a miracle... Now a Zeke turned up below him, and a Judy started a high overhead run. He broke out his guns and fired a short burst.

"Watch yourself!" he called to Caffey.

Caffey called back, "You watch 'em. I'm busy!"

Adams followed Harrison down and almost into the Kongo; he was less than half a mile away when he saw it. A hard left turn and a turn to the right took him between the battleship and two destroyers. All three opened fire on him. Adams thought, That stuff looks like flakes of tinfoil, and how I wish it was...

Kelly said, "Let's get out of here! They're firing from both sides of us!"

In a few minutes, Adams called back. "Well, we got through OK."

"Yeah," said Kelly, "but I don't see how we—"

"Hold it!" Adams told him. "We're not through yet. Here comes a Zeke!"

Kelly swung his guns. "I've still got a lot of fight left in me. Which side is he on?"

A brown Zeke was approaching from starboard, in a shallow high-side run. As Adams turned to meet him, the Zeke swept directly over his canopy. Neither plane fired. Ahead Adams saw a group of SBDs circling. Soon he could tell from the height of the numbers on their fuselages that they were Enterprise planes. One plane, with a number the size of his own, drew out and joined up on him. Adams recognized Jack Wright, from Bombing 16.

The day before, an oil leak had forced Wright to make an emergency landing on the nearest carrier in the force, the Enterprise. All planes aboard her were kept alerted, so he had no chance to rejoin the Lexington. He stayed there overnight, and when the Enterprise sent out her Air Group that afternoon — it was Air Group 10 — he asked permission to go along with the bombers. Their target was the Shokaku carrier. Twelve of them pushed over from 16,000 feet, with Wright next to the last. During the approach, the oil that had leaked into crevices in the nose of his plane had been pressed out by the propeller blast and smeared across his windshield. He couldn't see whether he made a hit, but Willie Fellows, his gunner, reported that the carrier was burning in several places.

Wright and Adams broke off from Bombing 10 to look for their own squadron. As they overtook a lone SBD, the pilot patted the side of his cockpit — the join-up signal — and turned hard to the left. Adams knew it was Hoggy Glacken, but didn't know that he was turning so sharply because a Zeke was making a run on them.

When Cushman pulled his heavy TBM out of its dive, he expected the AA to switch over to Buzzie Thomas, astern. It didn't. If anything, the volume of fire seemed to grow stronger. They're shooting everything they've got — maybe even rifles! One destroyer trained all its guns on him, but held its fire — the same destroyer that had let Kirkpatrick through a minute or two before. It was Cushman's only respite. However violently he twisted and zoomed, concussions still battered him. Two Zekes joined in. Between shellbursts, he tried to drive them off.

Thomas, the last plane down, turned southeast after Sterrie, but the TBMs had vanished. So had the SBDs. He had to fly the course alone and crippled. He knew the canopy over his center cockpit had blown out in the dive. Now he learned that the charging handle on Clasby's stinger-gun had broken in the pull-out. Stanfill thought of telling Clasby, "Your hand must have melted it off." Presently he had his own troubles. He ran out of ammunition, and the plane was jinking so sharply, he couldn't fit a fresh can into the holder. Clasby tried to help him, but the plane flung them from side to side.

The Zekes that had drawn the "Oh, Lord!" from Sterrie split into two groups of about eight apiece. The first group swarmed over Sterrie and Swanson until an F6F shot one down in flames and drove the rest away. The second group dove on Dupree, behind the TBMs, and Kirkpatrick, still farther behind.

Dupree's .50s had jammed. Now Dowdell's .30s jammed too. There was nothing he could do but call the passes as the Zekes attacked: "Coming in at eight o'clock!" or "Starboard side, five o'clock!", and Dupree would jerk the plane around to bring his cold guns to bear.

Once, with two Zekes coming in from different sides, Dowdell shouted only, "Start jinking!" Right then he suddenly remembered that today was his twentieth birthday.

Dupree's bluff worked. The Zekes broke off the attack. It had lasted ten minutes, but the only damage to his plane was one small hole in the trailing edge of his port wing — the first damage he had suffered in thirty-two combat missions.

Kirkpatrick had a rougher time. Two Zekes bored in on him from astern, with a third one on their tails. The first two shot away the top foot of his rudder and spattered bullets over the wing-roots and fuselage. The third one put an armor-piercing slug through his cockpit, peppering him with fragments of plexiglas and cutting a chip out of his starboard gun.

He dove to sea level where the gathering dusk would make him less conspicuous. The Zekes seemed to lose him for awhile, although he could see them plainly; they were taking positions for stern runs on Dupree. As the first one hovered, Kirkpatrick slid in beneath it, lifted the nose of his plane, and opened fire. At once two other Zekes whipped back in tight circles and blazed at him. He jinked to the water again, then crept back up for a shot at a fourth one, waiting its turn to make a pass.

He had climbed to 400 feet when the Japanese pilot, 200 feet higher, caught sight of him and hauled back his stick. Kirkpatrick and Bentley had the same thought: My God, he can't be trying a loop from there! They followed him around with their eyes, up, over, and down, 150 feet behind their tail in an almost vertical dive. Kirkpatrick kicked right rudder to watch the splash. The Zeke flattened out with feet to spare.

Bentley's voice was solemn. "Mr. Kirkpatrick, did you ever—"

Just then an F6F shot past them to port. Its tracers sparkled, and a Zeke curled into the ocean.

Moyers saw it splash. Another F6F flew by him a moment later and caught his "Stand by!" signal — bobbing the nose of his plane. It slowed down and began to weave above him. Soon three more F6Fs joined it; two of them seemed to have been shot up; their tail hooks were dangling. All four escorted him to the rendezvous.

Eight Zekes had peeled off on Weymouth, Shields and Sedell. Weymouth didn't think they would press the attack on his section. He expected them to swerve onto one of the stray planes near by, an easier, more helpless target. The first Zeke did not swerve. It came down in a 70° dive. All three gunners, McElhiney, LeMay and Maggio, had their .30s on it when it screamed past. Tony Maggio thought they had hit it, but even if they hadn't, he was certain it would never pull out from that low altitude. Instead, they saw what Kirkpatrick had seen. Tom Sedell thought, They handle like an oak-leaf in a windstorm, just like an oak-leaf!

The second Zeke broke its dive and pulled away. Then the third one came down...

Two miles to the north, Hoggy Glacken was leading Pinky Adams and Jack Wright in a tight circle to duck another Zeke. Adams' gunner, Harry Kelly, watched the first two runs on Weymouth's section and saw the third Zeke start its dive. Just then a strange plane loomed astern. Kelly picked up his microphone: "Plane approaching on our starboard quarter!"

Adams answered, "It's OK. It's Jack." Wright had fallen behind in the turn and was rejoining.

When Kelly looked back to Weymouth's section, only two SBDs were left. There was no foam on the water to show where the other one had gone, no flame, no smoke, nothing.

The third Zeke had started its run on Weymouth, but slid off to Shields and fired one burst as it darted between them. Tom Sedell had roomed with Jay Shields for two and a half years, ever since they had enlisted. He saw Shields stiffen back in his cockpit. His goggles flew off, and he looked as if he were screaming. Then he slumped over the stick, pushing it forward, and the plane nosed down. LeMay kept firing until the splash rose around him.

McElhiney sobbed, I could have cracked that Jap son of a bitch with a baseball bat, he was that close! I could have beat his dirty brains out!

The fourth Zeke had started its run. Weymouth and Sedell turned into it and beat it off, and the fifth one.

Singly and by twos and threes, the planes were converging on the rendezvous point — Bombing and Torpedo 16's, planes and planes from other air groups. Sedell signaled Weymouth to climb a bit higher, for more protection. Orv Cook overhauled them and joined up as Number 2, in Jay Shields's place. Slightly astern, Conklin joined up on Cleland's wing. The Zekes were using the Luftberry circle — diving out, attacking, and rejoining in turn. Cleland counted eighteen Zekes with only four F6Fs to oppose them. He couldn't understand why they concentrated on Weymouth's section, instead of on a cripple like himself. Conklin thought, Conk, old boy, you're just plain as lucky as hell!

Then the F6Fs began to gather, their airscoops whistling as they dashed into the fight. They were strangers, none of them from Fighting 16. One Zeke smoked, flamed, and fell 2000 feet, end over end. Another simply dropped its nose and glided into the water. The rest seemed to hesitate. As Dupree swung into place, he saw them scatter and run.

Kirkpatrick was the last to join. He was grinning, with a finger stuck through the hole in his canopy. Conklin showed him the hole.in his own canopy, and Cleland pointed to the long rip in his starboard wing. Caffey saw them; he almost regretted that he had no such trophies to display.

Weymouth did not wait for the different groups to filter out. He could not spare the fuel. He knew that his own squadron would follow him, forming as they flew. A course was ready for them. He had started preparing it when he was only a few seconds out of his dive, in the midst of the AA and the Zekes — jotting down data on the last maneuvers before the pushover, estimating his speed and his base course to the rendezvous, projecting his course to home. He touched his rudder lightly until his compass read 100°, then steadied off. The time was 7:18. It was hard for him to believe that since he had pushed over the Japanese fleet, only fourteen minutes had passed.

Three hundred yards to starboard the TBMs were forming. Cushman wasn't sure whether Sterrie knew which of his planes had been shot down. He drew alongside, held up six fingers, then one, and made a spiral motion toward the sea.

Sterrie glanced at his knee pad. Cushman could read his lips: "Sixty-one... McLellan..."

Sterrie looked up again, shaking his head slowly.

4

Air Group 16 had scheduled thirty-three planes for the attack: eleven F6Fs, seven TBMs, and fifteen SBDs. Four planes had turned back: two F6Fs, one TBM, and one SBD, but another SBD had joined up. Three planes had been shot down: an F6F, a TBM, and an SBD. The fighter pilot, Brockmeyer, was dead. The bomber crew, Shields and LeMay, were also dead. The torpedo crew, McLellan, Greenhalgh, and Hutchinson, were probably dead. All three had jumped from their burning plane, but Thomas had seen only one parachute open, and that one would drift into the Japanese fleet.

The twenty-seven surviving planes started their long flight home. The sun had set. Ahead of them, the sky would soon be dark.

5

The reason Thomas saw only one parachute open from McLellan's plane was that McLellan and John Hutchinson, his turret gunner, did not pull their rip cords until they had fallen several thousand feet. Neither of them ever saw the Zeke that shot them down; nor did Selbie Greenhalgh, the radioman. The Zeke attacked from astern, below, and McLellan's only warning was a spurt of tracers close to his canopy. Instinctively he jerked the stick to dodge, but fire had already burst from the gasoline filler pipe and was flooding the cockpit.

As he fumbled for his microphone to tell the crew to jump, a lick of flame seared his left wrist, between the cuff and the glove, and he snatched his hand away. He reached again, but the mike was gone. He looked back. By now fire had spread to the whole center cockpit. He was glad to see it, because it would tell Grenhalgh and Hutchinson what they had to do. He did not worry about them again. The three of them had been shot down together at Palau, and he knew that the other two could take care of themselves.

He opened the buckle of his safety-belt, holding his head over the side to catch a breath away from the choking smoke, then stood up in his seat and leaned out and tried to push off. The slipstream ripped away his helmet but plastered him to the edge of the canopy. He put his left foot against the instrument panel and shoved. Inch by inch he shouldered his way through the solid wall of wind. Presently it collapsed, and he shot beneath the tail, tumbling over and over. As he fell, the other planes seemed to be below him, flying upside down. Something's wrong here, he thought. I don't get it...

When McLellan jerked the stick, the plane jumped so violently that Greenhalgh and Hutchinson thought it had been hit in the belly by a heavy shell. Greenhalgh was buckling on his chute when Hutchinson slipped down into the tunnel. They saw that the whole forward fend was on fire, but Greenhalgh felt as if he had a world of time.

"Say, Hutch—" he began. He wanted to congratulate him on getting down for the first time without snagging his straps, but just then

McLellan's body hurtled past the window, and Hutchinson yelled, "Let's get out of here! This thing's going to blow!"

The escape hatch stuck until Hutchinson kicked it out. Greenhalgh went first. The slipstream caught him before he was clear and slammed him against the fuselage, with his legs bent around the jamb. Hutchinson pried him loose and jumped after him. Greenhalgh pulled his ripcord at once. He watched the burning plane fly levelly, then begin to climb. He could hear its motor screaming. Funny how shrill it is, he thought, just like a woman! And then it nosed down, trailing a long cloak of flames, and he never saw it again.

McLellan and Hutchinson grabbed their ripcords as soon as they were clear, but did not pull them. They wanted to fall through the antiaircraft bursts and out of the notice of Jap pilots, who might strafe them. Even so, McLellan pulled earlier than he had intended. Somersaulting down, he lost sight of the water and became afraid that he was falling too far. When the chute opened, he seemed to stop abruptly. He had no sense of downward motion. He felt only as if he were at the end of a gigantic pendulum, swinging from an invisible hook fixed far overhead. He tugged on his risers until the swinging stopped.

He thought, There's no hurry. I don't have to go down until I'm ready… The ripcord handle: they say nobody ever saves 'em, but I'll save this one. He tried to stuff it into one of his pockets, but it was like stuffing a lively spring. Presently he thought, What am I doing this for? Why would I be needing a ripcord handle? and let it fall.

Now he looked around him. Two other parachutes were close by. He was trying to make out which was which when a dogfight started overhead. He could hear the sound of the guns and the pop of the bullets as they shot past him. The pops were so loud, he wondered if he was being strafed. He craned back for a look. His view was screened by the canopy, but at least there were no bullet holes in it. Below, a Zeke was strafing something on the water. It made McLellan mad to think that maybe it was his own plane.

The pendulum-swing had started again. By the time he stopped it, the ocean had begun rushing up toward him. There were only a few seconds before he would hit. He undid the chest-buckle of his chute, and the left hip-buckle, and pulled the little lanyard that would inflate the left side of his life jacket. Just as he plunged in, he undid the right hip-buckle and squirmed out of his harness. He rose to the surface quickly. Nothing to fear: the water's warm, and in half a minute I'll be snugged down in my raft.

The back pack, loaded with survival and rescue equipment, was strapped over his shoulders, and the raft pack was attached to the parachute itself. McLellan knew exactly what he had to do. He had been trained in the routine until it had become automatic, and he had put it into practice that time at Palau: Hold the raft pack with your right arm, and reach under the life jacket and undo the buckle of the back pack...

But the routine went wrong. The life jacket kept shoving his face into the water, and the more he struggled, the more his gloves peeled down and interfered with his fingers. It took a long time to work the wet gloves off. The parachute had started to sink. He could feel its pull becoming heavier. The chest buckle was stubborn. He cursed it and snatched-the knife from his shoulder holster and sawed at the thick strap across his left shoulder until the back pack came free.

Now keep the raft pack under your right arm, and tuck the back pack under your left arm, and get that knife into its sheath. He clipped it in at last. Now the other buckle — the one that held the chute to the raft. His fingers felt as if he were still wearing gloves, and the sinking chute made it harder and harder to catch a breath. He had to kick himself to the surface, gulp in air, and go down again, feelingly blindly for a buckle that wasn't where it should be. Cut it away! He took out his knife again, but before he could use it, the chute broke from his grip with live strength. He fought back to the surface and inflated the other side of his life jacket and wiped the salt from his eyes. He was putting away his knife when he realized that the raft was gone forever.

Up to that moment, McLellan had not been really frightened, but now he remembered what a staff officer had announced just before they took off: "Anybody who's shot down we'll pick up, if they're in a boat."

If they're in a boat... A night in a raft is no night at the Ritz, but at least it keeps you fairly dry, and you can relax until a search plane spots you. But in a life jacket, your chin is only an inch or two out and only part of the time. A life jacket is something different — something very different in shark waters...

Hutchinson's raft was gone, too. So was Greenhalgh's. Neither of them had hooked the safety clasp before he jumped, and the rafts tore loose when the chutes snapped open. Greenhalgh watched the package fall. All his hopes fell with it... A guy can't last in just a life-jacket. He'll drown before they pick him up. Don't even think about it! There's a big show going on below. Think about that instead. Watch it! It's the last show I'll see, so I'll try to see it all...

It was quite a show to watch. He saw one big carrier take a hit just forward of the island, and a near miss. A covey of SBDs swung close to his chute, but veered away when they realized that they were attracting anti-aircraft fire to him. Another big carrier began to burn and list. He was watching it, spellbound, waiting for it to capsize, when his feet were knocked from under him, and water rushed into his mouth and nose, and the shrouds of the chute tangled around his neck. He choked and vomited before he could cut them away and inflate his life jacket. When the nausea passed, and his eyes cleared, he looked for McLellan and Hutchinson, who should be near by, but he couldn't see them because of the tossing waves. Instead, he saw a Japanese heavy cruiser passing 200 feet away.

He also saw something else even more terrifying: the fall had burst one of his dye-markers, and the brilliant green stain was spreading around him. Despite it, the cruiser ignored him. So did three Zekes which flew close overhead.

McLellan was so directly in the cruiser's course that he saw only its bow and beam. It was less than 100 yards off when it made a sharp turn that would bring it by to his right. The green side of his life jacket was outward, and he kept perfectly still in the water, hoping he wouldn't be seen. The Jap sailors did not even glance in his direction; they were watching the crippled carrier. Lousy discipline, McLellan thought. Look at 'em standing around on the decks and turrets when they ought to be at their battle stations! If we ever did that on the Lex—! He was surprised to see that they were in khaki, except for one man in whites. Probably a mess cook; he's about where the galley would be. Two stacks, both raked; Nachi class... Then the cruiser was gone, and he was being buffeted by its wash.

Two battleships crossed the cruiser's course. Zekes were circling one of the Hayataka carriers, but it was heading downwind, with thick black smoke pouring from its stacks, and it did not turn to take them aboard. The attack was still raging somewhere, because McLellan could feel the concussions through the water — quick, sharp blows against his stomach. He tried floating on his back, but the throbs made his ear-drums ache. He forgot them when another carrier came over the horizon. He could see it clearly — a Shokaku. Fire and smoke spilled from every vent. The whole flight deck seemed to be burned away. The ship flamed brighter and brighter against the darkening sky, then the forward end blew up. Fire shot 300 feet high and died to a glow. In half an hour, the glow went out. No smoke hung in the air. The huge ship left no trace. Even the concussions stopped. A few Jap planes passed by, but soon they disappeared into the dusk.

McLellan looked at his hands. They were pale and puckered. He shouted once for Greenhalgh and Hutchinson, but there was no answer.

6

When Alex Vraciu's first tour in the Pacific was finished, and his squadron was ready to go home, he asked permission to stay out for an extra tour. But when Brock-meyer was killed, Vraciu felt as if he never wanted to fight again. He had lost his wingman, lost the fighters, lost the bombers, and torpedo planes he was supposed to guard. He thought bitterly, I'll get credit for a sure and a probable, but I don't deserve credit for anything. Brock's gone, and I've fouled up the works...

He found a lone TBF, flying East, and moved in on its wing. There was a hole in the left side of its fuselage, its bomb-bay doors were open, and its engine was coughing. Vraciu saw a small "3" painted on its tail, but he did not know which air group used that style of lettering. After a few miles the pilot signaled, "How is your gas?" Vraciu answered with a thumb-up, then, "How's yours?" The pilot spread his hands and shrugged.

The other fighters were as despondent as Vraciu. They had not only lost the fight; they had also lost the enemy. Whiteway and Bartol, along with Arquette, never saw a Zeke all afternoon. They cruised over the northern formation, searching, still thinking it was Air Group 16's target, but all they saw was flames from the Shokaku carrier. Kosciusko and Seyfferle dove on a straggling destroyer and strafed it, but no Zekes took up their challenge. Sey-bert and Wendorf saw a Zeke duck into a cloud and tried to block its escape, but it did not come out on their side.

After an empty half-hour, the fighters began to straggle home. They were disorganized, apprehensive, and dispirited. No section knew where the others were. No pilot had much confidence in his navigation. None had any pride in what he had done that day.

7

Some thirty miles ahead of the fighters, the assortment of planes that had left the rendezvous together was separating into three formations. Torpedo 16's five TBMs were in the center, compact. To port were Bombing 16 and scattered strangers. The starboard group was mongrel — SBDs, TBMs, TBFs, F6Fs, and SB2Cs, from several different carriers.

At first they all followed Weymouth's lead. One of the strangers went on the air to say, "I don't know the guy who's taking us home, but I certainly like the way he's doing it!"

Sterrie wasn't so content. Weymouth was holding a course about 5° north of his own. We'd all have more confidence if we hung together, Sterrie thought, but I plotted my course carefully before dark, and I'm not going to change it now. Gradually the formation drew apart.

Meanwhile, the men were settling down. Weymouth made a crisp report to the base: four carriers seen hit, other ships probably damaged. Pinky Adams stretched back and took a deep tug at his water bottle. Kirkpatrick had jotted on his chartboard the numbers of the planes in the squadron; now he cruised around, squinting to identify them in the dusk, and circling each number as he found it. He found them all but Jay Shields'.

Tom Bronn, on Sterrie's wing, was checking his instruments. Suddenly he saw a danger sign: his oil pressure had jumped from 80 to 90. He reported it to Sterrie over the high frequency phone, with a warning that he might have to drop out at any moment. Linson, Bronn's radioman, heard the report and called him on the intercom. Bronn did not answer. He could receive Linson, but couldn't transmit to him. The shell that smashed their bomb-bay after the dive had smashed part of the intercom system.

Linson crawled forward to the center cockpit and handed Bronn a pad on which he had written, "Heard about oil pressure. If you want us to bail out, blink arm-master-switch 3 times, or twice to get set for water landing."

The arm-master-switch shows a red light in the tunnel.

Bronn wrote, "OK. Oil pressure up and engine acting up. Be ready for anything."

Linson crawled back to the tunnel and pushed the pad up to Banazak, in the turret. Banazak turned on his light, read the message and handed it back with a thumbs-up: "Understood."

The tropic night fell swiftly. The rendezvous point was only ten minutes astern when the planes began to turn on their lights, to avoid collisions. Oil had leaked across the front panels of Harrison's windshield; he had to drop slightly below the formation to be able to watch Weymouth's lights and his wingmen's. Over in the TBMs, oil had also smeared the turret of Thomas' plane; Stanfill, the gunner, could see nothing to port at all. He tried to take comfort from the fact that they were tail-end-Charlie.

Kirkpatrick had led the second division of SBDs to the attack, but he had been the last to join up at the rendezvous. He was trailing the squadron, with Conklin on his starboard wing. When the Zekes shot away part of Kirkpatrick's tail, they shot out his tail light. Conklin noticed it now and signaled him. Kirkpatrick signaled back that Conklin had no starboard wing light, and for him to change over so that his blind side would be between them. Together they pulled wide, where they would be less dangerous to the others.

Irish Caffey knew that home was eastward, but when the lights went on, he half wished that they were flying west. Ahead it's too dark. There's trouble ahead. Behind us it's brighter, with the last of the sunset and the fires from the Jap ships...

Presently, on the starboard beam, it was brighter still. From one of the tankers they had ignored on the way out, a red flame leaped up, mile-high. Someone else had not ignored them.

Seybert and Wendorf saw the explosion, and cut across to identify it. The tanker was already settling by the stern, and three others were afire. Seybert thought, There are our boys now! He picked up his microphone: "Forty-one Gimlet, Forty-one Gimlet! This is Five Gimlet. What is the position of the rendezvous point? Over."

Weymouth's voice came back: "This is Forty-one Gimlet. We departed for base ten minutes ago. Out."

Seybert's anger flared. He searched around, cursing. I've seen the Jap fleet and I haven't fired a God-damned shot! What's become of those Zekes? Where is everybody? There was no other plane but Wendorf's, on his wing. They circled once, on the last chance of finding an enemy, then started home together.

The air was busy with discussion of the proper course. Seybert listened awhile and made a mental average of the various recommendations: 98°. He steadied off there at 135 knots, and sat back to wait. The hours in front of him did not concern him so much as the hours behind. Tension swung his spirits from exuberance to dejection. *I saw the Jap fleet and I'm getting home with a whole skin... That's true, but it wasn't because I didn't try... Sure, I tried, hut my job was to protect the SBDs and TBMs, and I lost 'em...*

His flight clothes were drenched with nervous sweat. He reached into his knee pocket for a cigarette. The package was an empty wad.

8

The lone TBF that Vraciu had joined up on began to behave queerly. It lost altitude and cut its speed until he had to drop his flaps to stay with it. He thought it was intending to make a water-landing, but although it was almost brushing the crests of the waves, it still trudged on. Then he saw something even queerer: seven planes circling aimlessly, making no attempt to continue the homeward course. When the TBF moved into the circle, Vraciu could only mark the location on his chartboard, and leave them.

Presently he had forgotten the lunatic planes. All he could think of was a long, cold drink of water. His thirst made him see the white enamel scuttlebutt near his room on the Lexington. He was leaning over it, his thumb pressing the lever, the jet spurting into his mouth…

Kosciusko and Seyfferle were the last fighters to leave the target area. As they turned eastward Kosciusko heard Whiteway, somewhere up ahead, call attention to a flight of eight SB2Cs and ask Arquette and Bartol if they wanted to follow them back or continue along as they were. Kosciusko knew there was a chance that the SB2Cs would run out of fuel. He picked up his microphone to warn Whiteway, but his transmitter was dead.

Whiteway had suggested following the bombers because he was navigating by thumb and wasn't too certain of his course. They decided to keep going. Their speed would get them home first, and they could land and clear the decks for slower planes behind. He led them into the brighter air at 7000 feet and settled down to 170 knots. Arquette figured they would be over the force at 8:30.

9

The burning tankers were the last diversion for the tired men in the SBDs and TBMs. The fighters didn't have to worry about fuel; their belly-tanks would get them home. But the other crews began to hear their thoughts pacing a solitary cell: Will the fuel last? Will it? Will it?...

In normal flight at economical cruising speed, a smooth-running TBM or SBD could make the required distance, but few of these planes were smooth-running. Most of them had been in combat, off and on, for ten months. Their engines were old and gas-greedy, some of them dangerously so. Nor was it a normal flight. First there was the climb to more than 10,000 feet with a bomb load. Then came the full-power jinking from the pull-out to the rendezvous, and full power takes twice as much fuel as cruising speed. Now they were not only bucking a 14-knot head wind, but when they reached the task force, there would be an indeterminate period of circling — again under full power, to meet the drag of lowered flaps and landing gear — before they could go aboard their ship.

The heaviest responsibilities were Weymouth's and Sterrie's, setting the course and the pace for their squadrons. They took them to 1000 feet as a safety-margin and throttled back to "automatic lean" for maximum economy of fuel, but even so there was not a pilot with them whose calculations were not wearing identical grooves: 300 miles to go... ground speed 120... that's 2½ hours... allow half an hour more, maybe forty-five minutes, to find the Lex and get into the circle and take my turn coming aboard. It's going to be close...

It was already close for some of the pilots from other groups, lost, and their fuel dwindling. Panicky or plaintive or defiant, their voices came over the air:

"I've got ten minutes of gas left, Joe. Think I'll put her down in the water while I've still got power. So long, Joe!"

"This is Forty-six Inkwell. Where am I, please? Somebody tell me where I am!"

Kirkpatrick thought, God knows I'd like to help you, but how can I? I don't know where you are! He turned down the volume on his receiver. If only they wouldn't wail! It's the wailing tone that gets you...

The voices kept on. "Can't make it, fellows! I'm going in. Look for me tomorrow if you get a chance, will you?"

"I'm running low and I'm not picking up the beacon. Where's home, somebody? I'm lost!"

Some of the voices came from helpless pilots, whose instruments had failed or had been shot away. Some came from novice pilots, whose inexperience cowered from the black flight. Some came from careless pilots, who had been so stimulated by the prospect of attacking the Japanese fleet that they had simply ignored the insistencies of fuel and navigation.

Sy Seybert heard five of them discuss their situation as matter-of-factly as if they were holding a business conference: Should each of them keep going to his last drop, or should they ditch together right then? They agreed to abide by majority opinion and took a formal vote. It was four-to-one for ditching.

"That's that!" said the chairman. "OK. Here we go!"

Soon a proud voice spoke: "I've got sixty gallons!"

A cruel voice: "You expect to get home on sixty gallons?"

There was no answer.

Tom Sedell saw two unidentified SBDs and a TBF glide down and disappear. A moment later there were three dim splashes.

A calm voice: "I've got five gallons left. I'm getting ready for a water-landing."

Another calm voice: "Well, I've got seventeen, but I might as well go in with you."

The first voice: "Thanks, pal. Much obliged. Ready?..."

Home was still an hour and a half away when heat lightning began to flicker in the northeast. An excited voice: "There's the task force now! I see the lights! Let's go to it! Come on!"

Two others thought it was gunfire. "Don't shoot!" they begged. "Don't shoot! We're friendly!"

Weymouth shut off his radio. He felt as if his life were being sapped away. Pinky Adams kept listening. So far nobody from Air Group 16 had asked for help or sympathy, and Adams had bet himself that they never would. Each minute of their restraint made him prouder.

Air Group 16's pilots and crews weren't talking even on the intercoms. Usually, on their way home, they discussed the attack or merely passed the time. Tonight they had little to say. Some were too exhausted. Others were afraid to spread the infection of their own fears. Only a few of the gunners and radiomen blurted out the question that was roweling each one's mind.

Stanfill to Thomas: "We going to have enough gas to get back?"

"Sure!" Thomas told him. "Sure, we'll get back!" He didn't add what he was thinking: *But it's going to be ticklish...*

Hisler to Cleland: "How we doing?"

"We'll be in the money." *What the hell — we got a hit; you can't have everything!*

Sample to Conklin: "How's our gas?"

Conklin's gauge was erratic. He could have made a fairly accurate estimate from the elapsed time, but his watch had stopped on the way to the target. He signaled Bentley, Kirkpatrick's gunner, and asked the time by hand-taps in Morse: fist for a dot, palm for a dash. Bentley signaled back, and Conklin reset his watch.

"We're in pretty good shape," he told Sample.

McElhiney to Weymouth: "Gas holding up OK?"

"We're doing pretty good."

Van Etten to Moyers: "Doesn't look like any of us are going to get home, does it?"

Moyers did not answer.

LeBlanc was about to call Swanson when he happened to glance toward Sterrie. *Hell, if Mr. Sterrie is as cool as all that, why should I fret?*

Barrett had a different anxiety. He asked Harrison, "Are we lost?"

"Of course we're not lost!" Less firmly, Harrison added, "If you want to worry, worry about all those planes that are going to be lousing up the landing circle when we get back!"

Orv Cook, on Weymouth's wing, wanted to ask him for an ETA, but *it'd just scare me if he told me. I'd better just hang on the best I can.* He made some trivial comment to LeMieux, but LeMieux had no small talk. He was busy praying.

Kirkpatrick and Bentley were quieter than they had ever been before. Kirkpatrick started to say something chatty, but he suddenly remembered the time when they were in their raft off Truk: *That cheer-up conversation of mine went over like a ten-day-old pancake, didn't it?*

Now physical fatigue and nervous strain began to take toll in a form that few of the men had ever experienced: vertigo. Darkness had shut down completely. There was no visible horizon, even in the west, and no moon. Low clouds occasionally obscured the stars. The only reference points were the small lights of the planes themselves, and the pattern of these was unstable. Some blinked on and off; some fell below and behind, as a pilot switched from an empty tank; some lights were missing altogether.

Kirkpatrick's tail light was gone, and Conklin, on his port wing, had no starboard wing light of his own. The two of them had pulled wide from the rest of the formation, and Kirkpatrick's port wing light was Conklin's only guide. There were moments when he couldn't tell whether it was fifty yards away or fifty inches. Twice he kicked his rudder just before their wing-tips swerved together. His sense of balance became numb. He began to doubt the evidence of his instruments, telling him that he was in level flight when he would have sworn that he was in a climbing turn. Thank God for Kirk! Look at him: steady as a rock! If I lose Kirk —

Kirkpatrick was flying by muscular memory. His artificial horizon was out of order, and vertigo was rushing over him in waves. He oriented himself on a star only to find that it was a light on another SBD, as faltering as his own. Bentley felt it. Once he thought that they were climbing straight up, and ripped out the cartridge screen to check his altimeter. Its needle was notched at 900 feet. He rapped the glass panel to make sure it wasn't stuck.

Seybert and Wendorf were flying at 4000 feet, an altitude that took them through the bottoms of the thunder-heads that had built up across their course. Wind currents tossed them and rain deafened them until Seybert became dizzy. He felt himself gaining speed. By the time he realized that he had slipped off in a long diving turn, he had fallen more than half a mile.

All the pilots, and the gunners in the SBDs and TBMs, could at least look around and get some reassurance from the lights of the other planes. But the radiomen in the TBMs were confined in tunnels, with no escape for their eyes. Not only vertigo found them there, but hypnosis, induced by the vibration. The bulkheads blurred and swayed out and in, expanding and contracting the enclosure. Klingbeil propped them with his hands. He was hunched in his seat with his nerves drawn doubly taut, against the deception of his senses and against the imminence of a disaster that would strike without warning — the explosion of silence that meant the last tank had run dry, or the shock of a crash into the sea.

Hypnosis rode with the pilots too, sitting alone in the darkness. Their engines beat out a rhythm, the rhythm became a drone, and the drone became a lullaby, stupefying and perilous.

Sterrie jerked back from the very edge of a trance. At once he drove himself into a frenzy of industriousness, shuttling his attention around the circuit of his cockpit, purposely complicating the simplest procedures — anything to keep another trance at bay. He twisted his head from side to side, so that his eyes would not be trapped by the glow of one instrument. He touched buttons and switches, eased his straps, patted his pockets. He made an elaborate ceremony of taking out his flashlight and examining his fuel gauge. When a tank runs dry, the engines stop, unless the pilot cuts in a fresh tank just as the needle begins to totter. Sterrie watched the needle for an instant, looked away, watched it again.

Wherever a pilot turned his eyes and however often, he always brought them back to that needle. SBDs have four tanks. By now the third was running dry. Some pilots did not see the needle fall in time to switch over smoothly. Their engines died, and their planes drifted down until fuel pumps brought them into place again. The formation was stretching and closing in the darkness.

Moyers switched over and called Van Etten: "Last tank…"

Adams let his engine suck the last few drops of fuel from his third tank. He switched and pumped it back to life, then called Kelly: "Next time you hear us run out of gas, you'll know we're going in the drink."

Kelly answered calmly, "Roger."

When Irish Caffey switched, he told himself, Fifty gallons left, and that's all. Well, hell! Well, hell!

Estrada heard their engine conk and catch. He knew what it meant, but he didn't care any more. He was tired out, tired of thinking about Shields and Brockmeyer and McLellan. He'd seen all three planes shot down.

And then they began to pick up the homing signal. Dupree was one of the first; he caught it about seventy-five miles out. Immediately he flashed a light on his chart-board, to check the sector. Ever since the rendezvous, he had been flying on a fuel-mixture leaner than the safe minimum. He knew it would burn out the engine if he used it long enough, but it saved a vital few gallons of gas an hour. For some time his engine had been spitting white sparks in warning; now it sputtered and nearly stopped. He dropped his flashlight and jumped for the throttle and mixture-control. When his exhaust cooled, he leaned the mixture again. But he couldn't find his flashlight.

It didn't matter whether everyone picked up the beacon so long as the leaders did. Sterrie caught it when he was sixty miles out. He and

Weymouth had both been holding courses a bit too far to the north. Now they swung to starboard and headed in on the beam, with their squadrons following.

Exactly at 8:30 they made their first visual contact with the task force, on a vertical searchlight from a ship in the Bunker Hill's group.

Conklin said aloud, "Boy, oh boy, what a relief! We're here!"

Buzzie Thomas told Clasby, "We're here! The force is right ahead!"

With only thirty gallons left, Pinky Adams hoped that Weymouth would head for the light. When he didn't, Adams told himself, We're back, anyway! If we go down, now, they'll pick us up.

When LeBlanc saw the light, he called Swanson. "How much gas left now?"

Swanson had about an hour's. "Two hours," he said. LeBlanc unlocked the hatch in the middle cockpit and wedged the handle so that it couldn't snap shut. He knew that their troubles were just beginning.

10

The carriers in Task Force 58 were spaced over hundreds of square miles of ocean. Each pilot had to find one of these carriers in the dark, and having found it, he had to execute without a fault the complicated routine of landing his plane.

Even in full daylight, this routine is difficult. It begins with the squadron circling at a safe altitude until the carrier has turned into the wind and has signaled, "I am ready to receive planes." As soon as the leader of the first section gets this signal, he shakes his wings for the "break-off," lowers his wheels and flaps, and drops down into the landing-circle, with his wingmen trailing him. The leader of the second section follows in line, and so on for the other sections.

The landing — "circle" is shaped like the rim of a bathtub, and its sides are called "legs." The first, the upwind leg, begins astern of the carrier, and leads past its starboard side. When the pilot has gained a mile or more, he turns to port, flies a crosswind leg of half a mile, and turns to port again. He is now entering his downwind leg, on a course reciprocal to the carrier's.

Opposite her stern, he begins another turn to port, on a curve tangent to her wake, and if he executes this last turn correctly, he finds himself "in the groove," overhauling her from dead astern. The closer he approaches, however, the more of the deck is screened by the nose of the plane, and it would be almost impossible for him to complete his landing without guidance during those last critical seconds.

A guide is there — the landing signal officer, whose job is one of the most important and most delicate on the entire ship. His station is a small platform on the after port quarter of the flight deck. Behind him is a square canvas panel, to shield him from the steady pressure of the wind across the deck and from the slipstream of a newly landed plane gunning its engine to taxi forward. Beside him is a narrow safety net, for him to dive into if a plane veers too close. If he should spill over the after edge of the net, he would fall six feet into a gun mount; over the forward edge, fifty feet into the sea.

Guiding a plane in, the signal officer uses a code of gestures emphasized by two bright-colored paddles or flags — arms forming a V if the plane is too high, or an inverted V if it is too low; arms horizontal if it is properly level, arms tilted if it is not. At the proper point in a correct approach, the signal officer draws his right hand across his throat: "Cut your engine and land." The pilot drops his plane to the deck, his tail-hook catches one of several parallel wires stretched athwartships, and he is dragged to a stop. If the approach is not satisfactory, the signal officer holds his paddles overhead, crossing and uncrossing them, as a "wave-off," and the pilot swerves to port and takes his turn in the landing circle again. A wave-off must be obeyed. A pilot who ignores it will be grounded.

The Lexington's landing signal officers were John Shuff and Eugene Hanson, both experienced pilots. The first of the returning planes appeared over the task force at 8:15. Until then, it had been steaming west, to close the distance to the target. As the ships turned east, into the wind, to take the planes aboard, Shuff and Hanson went aft to their station.

Hanson looked at the sky. "No moon tonight," he said. "That ought to fix us up proper."

Shuff said, "Moon or no moon, it would be a rat-race."

Each type of plane has to be landed in a different way, according to its characteristics. Sometimes different models of the same type require different handling. Air Plot had already notified Shuff and Hanson that these first planes were SB2Cs, a type which Air Group 16 did not include.

Shuff had landed only two of them, visitors, but Hanson had not had even this much experience. He told Shuff, "You know those babies. You might as well start out."

Shuff knew that SB2Cs had a tendency to float after their engines were cut, and that the earlier models had to come in five knots faster than the later ones, but he did not know how he was going to distinguish them in the dark. He stepped on the button that raised the windscreen behind him, switched on his fluorescent wands, and glanced across to the opposite corner of the ramp, to see if Bud Dering was at his post. Dering had two jobs: to warn Shuff when a plane was off line, too close to the island, and to put a spotlight on each approaching plane, to see if its tail-hook was properly extended. He blinked his red flashlight to show Shuff that he was ready.

The Lexington was steadying on her new course. Commander Southerland spoke into a microphone on the flight control bridge, and the bull-horn sent his voice thundering over the flight deck: "Land planes!"

Twice during the early part of the evening Admiral Mitscher had left flag plot for the flag bridge. Both times he had stood there alone, staring at the sky. The staff knew his dilemma and knew that only he could make the choice: Turn on the lights and risk the ships? Or leave them off and risk the pilots?

He had brought thousands of men and a billion dollars worth of ships into enemy waters. Five nights ago, enemy planes had dropped four torpedoes at the Lexington, and two of them had passed within ten yards of her hull. The Lexington had been blacked out then. If she and the other ships were lit up now, any torpedo plane or bomber or submarine in the area could hardly miss. On the other hand, night landings were hazardous enough under full lights. Some of the pilots now aloft had never made a night landing, and even the best pilots were out of practice. The prospect of several hundred planes fumbling for those narrow decks in the dark —

Mitscher returned to flag plot and dropped onto the leather couch. For a minute or two, he smoked in silence. Then he pushed back his cap and rubbed his forehead. "Turn on the lights," he said.

Captain Burke sent the order over the TBS, and searchlights flashed on, some vertical as signposts to the force, some horizontal as signposts to the carriers. Low clouds stunted a few of the vertical beams, but the rest were in the clear.

The first plane was dead astern. Shuff caught it with his wands, lowered it slightly, held it, then drew the right wand across his throat. The hook caught the second wire, and a big plane crunched to the deck, its wheels smoking and its tail bucking against the counterweights that dragged it to a stop. It was not an SB2C, but a TBF. The time was 8:50.

"That's one of 'em in, anyhow," Shuff said.

The plane had hardly stopped when a deck crew freed its hook and waved the pilot to taxi to the bow. There had been only a few seconds' interruption in his forward movement. No more could be allowed. The next plane was already coming up the groove.

Mitscher asked, "Whose plane was that?"

"The Hornet's, sir."

"Hornet? She's not even in our task group. If the boys are having that much trouble finding their ships, we might as well tell them to land wherever they can. Just so we get them down tonight, we can unscramble them tomorrow morning."

The pilots heard it at 8:52. "All planes, from Commander Task Force 58. Land on any base you see."

Shuff brought in the second plane, a strayed F6F, then almost at once — as Mitscher's order took effect — he wished he were on a dim little "jeep," or any carrier except the large, well-lit Lexington. He felt as if he were under a strafing attack. Instead of the orderly file that should have been approaching him, pairs of planes, even groups, roared up the groove together, elbowing and jockeying for his favor.

It was impossible to single out one of them. The pilot beside it or above it might mistake the signals as meant for himself, and if two of them attempted a simultaneous landing, both planes would be wrecked, both crews would be killed, and the deck would be fouled up for an hour. Shuff waved them all away. He realized bitterly that among them might be planes with wounded men aboard and planes with insufficient gas to make the circuit again, but there was no help for it.

He waved off the next group and the next, landed an Enterprise F6F, and waved off another group. The 24-inch wands, loaded with electric batteries, were dragging at his arms, and still the clotted groups came on, thicker and thicker yet. He landed a third F6F and picked up another TBF. It was almost at the ramp when its engine conked, the port wing dropped, and its tip swung toward Shuff's chest like a seven-ton scythe. He dove into the net and lifted his head in time to see the splash. Three dim figures crawled out. They waved as they fell astern.

Only ten minutes had passed since Shuff had landed the first plane, but the pilots' anxiety had already risen to desperation. Earlier they had accepted his wave-offs at once, but now they were boring in to the very edge of the ramp, apparently hoping that their rivals would quit at the last second. As a result, some of them skimmed over the deck so low that time after time Shuff had to snap down the canvas screen behind him, or they would never have cleared it. Others pulled up straight over the flight deck. Still others cut to starboard, almost scraping their wing tips on the 5-inch turrets aft of the island.

Dering gave up using his red flashlight. He simply yelled across the deck, "Wave him off! Wave him off! He's way over here!"

Every man on the ship who was off duty that night had come topside to watch the show. They were clustered on the island, along the catwalks, on the bridges and searchlight platforms, even in the 40-millimeter tubs.

When the first few planes were waved off, they had called, "Never mind! You'll catch the brass ring next time!" But soon they fell quiet. Planes that landed safely were cheered all the way up the deck, but nobody joked any more; few of them even talked. When the TBF splashed in, a bos'n's mate said, "Nobody ordered me to watch this. I'm going below."

Two other men followed him.

Shuff brought in a fourth F6F and waved away a group at his heels. One of them plunged into the water. He thought it was a fighter and he thought he saw the pilot bob up, but he wasn't sure. His sixth plane was an SB2C. Still no plane from Air Group 16 had come aboard. Another group was starting up the groove. As they melted away with a wave-off, they revealed a plane behind them — a plane with no lights, flying fast, straight for the ramp. Shuff waved his wands. A plane that hit the deck at such a speed would tear out the whole barrier system, and the Lexington could not land another plane that night. The blind plane did not swerve or slow.

Midway up the flight deck stood Lieutenant (j.g.) Verne Prather, the chief of the flight deck crews. He saw the plane that was driving in, and he crouched like a football player, ready to spring.

Shuff waved again, frantically and more frantically.

Past Prather, up at the bow, Plane Handling Crew Number 6 was securing the SB2C that had just landed. An aviation machinist's mate, William Long, stood in front of it, beckoning it forward the last few feet into its parking space. Two men stooped close to its wheels, waiting to chock them with heavy wooden cradles when Long gave the signal. Eight more men were pushing on the wings, helping to fold them.

As the rogue plane shot past Shuff, Commander Southerland spun the handle of the crash siren. Prather yelled, "Clear the deck!" and fell flat, an instant before a wing tip slashed at his head. Long yelled, "Six get clear! Six get clear!" Some of his crew managed to roll into the cat-walks. Some flung themselves down and wrapped their arms around their faces. The chockmen held their posts. So did Long.

The rogue plane struck with a grinding crash. Every light on the deck went out. A bubbling scream broke through the blood in somebody's throat. Somebody shouted, "Loose bomb!" And then there was no sound but the hissing of the fire extinguishers.

Prather was already sprinting forward. Close behind him ran Dr. Neal Baxter, the air group's flight surgeon, with two corpsmen and two stretcher bearers. A green spotlight flashed down from the bridge. One of the corpsmen stopped dead and whispered, "Mary, Mother of Jesus!", then followed Prather and Baxter into the hot tangle.

The six planes that Shuff had brought aboard had been parked at the bow: four F6Fs, a TBF, and an SB2C. Two of the F6Fs were on the starboard side, out of the way. The other four planes stood in the direct line of the crash. Rearmost was the SB2C which Shuff had just landed. Its pilot and gunner were still in their seats, waiting for the wheels to be chocked. The rogue's propeller sliced through the rear cockpit and cut the gunner in half. The tail assembly was telescoped into the front end, pinioning the pilot, and the whole mass slammed into the three planes ahead, completely destroying them as well.

One of the chockmen was mashed to death. Long was unconscious with a concussion. Four other crewmen were injured. The pinioned pilot had a crushed foot. The pilot and the gunner of the rogue plane were unhurt. It was another SB2C, a wing-plane of the plane it had struck.

Prather scrambled onto its wing and reached into the pilot's cockpit to make sure that the switches were off, and ordered the batteries disconnected. Oil and gasoline from the shattered tanks had gushed across the deck and splashed into the portside catwalk and gun mounts. A single stray spark, and wildfire would wrap the ready ammunition.

Baxter dragged out the injured men, bandaged them, and gave them morphine. Long, in his delirium, was moaning, "Six get clear! Six get clear!" The acid light made the dead men's blood as black as tar.

An ensign in one of the 5-inch gun mounts was wiping oil from his eyes when he felt someone tug his elbow. A crewman in earphones was mouthing at him, but no words came. Finally the crewman simply pointed. A 250-pound bomb, fused, had come to rest a few feet away.

Prather stumbled and slithered around the heap of planes, estimating how long it would take to break them apart and shove them over the side. The powerful deck crane had already trundled forward and was waiting. Prather gave instructions to its crew, then ran back to the island and shouted up to Southerland, "Ten minutes!"

Southerland shouted back, "Do your best!"

The moment the SB2C crashed, Southerland had pulled the masterswitch on the light panel, to black out the ship and warn planes that her deck was foul. None could be landed until the wreckage was removed, and every minute's delay brought them nearer to the imminent exhaustion of their fuel.

He glanced at the sky. Even the semblance of a landing circle had vanished. Planes were stampeding in an animal panic, blind and headlong, crowding and shoving to be the first in line when the Lexington's lights went on again. They seemed to hover over the stem until the last split-second before a stall, then they would spurt away and circle back into position. Four minutes passed. The crane dipped into the junk-pile again and wrenched. Something came free, dangled over the side of the ship, and splashed. Five minutes. An SBD skittered along the waves only a hundred feet off the port beam, then stopped abruptly and sank. No one got out. Another plane went in, too far astern for Southerland to identify it. Eight minutes. Nine…

Prather's voice bellowed up, "Let 'er go!"

The SB2C had crashed at 9:10. At 9:20, the Lexington's lights went on again. Shuff picked up his wands. A lone TBF was coming up the groove. He gestured it downward, slowed it a few knots, and brought it in. When he looked back to the groove, six planes were hurtling toward him. The stampede had resumed.

11

It was in full cry when the planes of Air Group 16 began to trail across the screen. The fighters were the first. They had heard Mitscher's permission to land on any base, but most of them felt as Jim Seybert did: I want my own signal officer to bring me in to my own ship, so I can sleep in my own sack! They had been fairly confident that once they found the task force, they could find their own task group, and the Lexington. Their confidence faded when they saw the scene below them.

Two dim red bulbs, the truck lights, showed on each ship's foremast, but whether they marked a carrier or a cruiser, a pilot could guess only by their altitude, and too often he did not know his own. Each carrier burned a glow light, a foot square and individual in color, but it could be seen only from dead above, and although the flight decks were pricked out by tiny bulbs, they were visible only from close astern.

The pilots saw them in glimpses, when they saw them at all. Between glimpses they were blinded. Starshells were bursting in a dazzling glare. Searchlights flashed on and off. Flares blazed from the water, marking the spot where someone had plunged. And through the confusion flickered the lights of the planes themselves, red and green and white and yellow, swarming through the air, bobbing and weaving and crisscrossing like neon confetti in a whirlwind.

Seybert and Wendorf split apart four times to let stray planes slip between them. They spotted a carrier, lost it, and lost another. A formation of bombers rushed at them head on, driving them almost into the water. Seybert began to talk down his rising panic. Damn you, you've been flying these things, for quite a while now! You can get aboard! Just keep your head! Now get in-there and pitch!

He found another carrier, dropped his flaps, and shook his wings to warn Wendorf. He was in the groove on his first approach, when a plane with no lights suddenly appeared to port, and he had to pull up to starboard so quickly that his wing tip missed the island by inches. The second time around, he was making his last turn when a searchlight beam showed him that he was only ten feet above the water. He zoomed up, overshot the groove, and came in too high and too fast. He saw the wave-off, but veered away to starboard — Why did I do that? — straight over the island again. He snatched his stick and crouched over it, waiting for the rip and shock of his tail-hook catching the radio antenna. The ship was a mile astern before the knotted muscles of his belly would relax.

He was halfway around on his next approach when three things happened at once: a voice in his earphones shouted, "Get set for a hell of a hard landing!", the ship turned off all its lights, and he noticed that his fuel gauge was stuck. He tried to talk down a new assault of panic: Take it easy, Seybert! Easy now,! Easy! The ship's lights came on again, but the plane in front of him tangled itself in the barrier, fouling the deck, and he was waved off. Easy, Seybert! Easy now!

He braced himself against the back of his seat and started his fifth approach. The signal officer gave him a cut. He saw two familiar turrets and knew it was the Lexington. He didn't want to taxi forward; he wanted to jump from his cockpit and kiss the deck.

Someone called, "Here's old Seybert! Hey, Sy!" and pounded his shoulders. He couldn't understand it until they told him that he was the only fighter who had landed aboard.

"Where's Wendy?" he asked. "He ought to have been here long ago! Where is he?"

No one could tell him.

12

When Seybert shook his wings, Wendorf waited until he had enough interval, then lowered his wheels and started his turn into the downwind leg. Suddenly he saw two pale blue flames streaming toward his starboard wing — exhaust flames from a plane with no lights. If he tightened his turn, he would mush into a collision. He shoved his stick forward, saw the blind plane's wheels sweep four feet over his canopy, and hauled the stick back again. It was too late. His left wheel struck the water, then his left wing-tip. The Hellcat leaped forward, wing over wing, in a series of giant cartwheels. Wendorf lost consciousness on the third one.

13

 Kosciusko knew he was closing the task force, and still he received no buzz from the homing beacon. The damn thing's conked, he thought, just when I need it most! His transmitter was also dead. He tried to signal Seyfferle to take over the lead by blinking the lights on his turtleback, but Seyfferle did not understand. Neither did any of the ten planes that had joined up on the way. They flew on, apparently confident that he had a bee-line for home.
 The signal finally came in just in time. Flying at 7000 feet, he ran into a storm that tossed his plane until the instruments on his panel bobbed and danced. He dropped to 1000 feet, but the storm seemed to have no bottom, so he decided to climb over it. When he reached smooth air, only four planes were still with him. Now the signals came in strongly. He followed them down and broke through the clouds directly over the Hornet's crowded landing circle. He saw Seyfferle head for it, but Kosciusko couldn't wait for the circle to thin; his fuel was getting too low. He found another carrier and came aboard after two wave-offs. As his tail-hook caught, his canopy slammed shut and locked. He thought, If that had been a water-landing, my friend!...

14

Whiteway brought his section, Bartol and Arquette, home at 8000 feet. Arquette had estimated that they would pick up the task force at 8:30, and it was approximately then that they first saw lights flashing and altered course toward them, 10° south. The flashes were from lightning, but before they realized it, they had crossed the task force, its lights blanketed by the thick, low clouds, and were miles beyond it.

Whiteway turned northeast. He was flying on instruments, with Bartol and Arquette flying contact on his wings. Their lights and his own were mirrored by his glass canopy, and were broken into dazzling sparkles by the clinging drops of rain. He called them, trying to tell them to move further apart, but his transmitter was out of order, and they could not understand his signals.

A starshell burst near him, searing his eyes. He began to feel as if he were flying inside a gigantic electric bulb. A black cloud enveloped him, but another starshell burst inside the cloud and blinded him completely. His last glimpse of his instruments showed him that he was only three knots above a spin. When he saw them again, he had fallen more than a mile. Another wave of dizziness surged over him and he fell off in another dive. When he brought the plane under control, his altimeter showed only 200 feet. His eyes began to clear. He could see a few stars, but Bartol and Arquette were gone.

By now Whiteway was completely lost. His transmitter was out; so was his receiver. There was nothing to do but fly an expanding spiral in hope of finding a carrier before the last of his fuel burned away. An hour had passed since he had been deceived by the lightning flashes. As the probability of a water-landing became stronger, he took off all his gear except his life-jacket and slid back the canopy. The spiral took him in and out of rain clouds. His wet clothes clung to his body.

Suddenly he saw a searchlight. It seemed close by, but he had flown for ten minutes before he could see that it was from a destroyer. Five miles further was another searchlight. He was half way toward it when red truck lights blinked beneath his wing, and a carrier's deck lights flashed on. An SB2C was already in the landing circle. Whiteway followed it around and came aboard. He had 15 gallons, enough for one more pass. The time was 9:50. The ship was a light carrier. It had to push the SB2C over the side to make room for Whiteway's F6F.

14

For Johnny Bartol, the most terrifying moment of the whole flight was when he flew into a cloud with Whiteway and Arquette and came out alone. Until then, he had simply followed Whiteway's lead. Now he had to navigate for himself, to trust his own instruments, and to coordinate what they told him.

He climbed to 16,000 feet, then glided back, searching for the homing beacon. At 12,000 feet it came in loud enough to give him a bearing: he was southeast of the task force. He approached it on a long slant. Three fighters from another air group joined him. They were lost, they said, and suggested that they all bail out together.

Bartol asked, "How's your gas?"

"We've got about 75 gallons apiece."

"Hell, that'll get you home. Just stick with me."

Five minutes later he saw the glow of a searchlight beam through a cloud, and below it he found a carrier.

"Go ahead," he told the others. "I've got 10 gallons more than you have."

He tailed them into the landing circle. The first two strangers swept aboard, but the third crashed into a barrier and fouled the deck. Bartol could not chance its clearing quickly; he had to find another carrier. The Bunker Hill was near by, but there was a fire on her deck. The next carrier — he couldn't identify her — had a crash. Finally he picked up the Wasp, with an empty circle. He landed there at 9:45, the first plane to get aboard that night.

The sight of Whiteway peeling off in his dizzy spin increased Jim Arquette's own dizziness. He had vertigo; he was lost; he doubted whether he could make the necessary change from contact-flying to instruments. He was considering bailing out, and was praying for help and guidance, when the dizziness began to pass, and the homing beacon gave him a course of 350°. Thirty miles along, a searchlight beam pointed to the Bunker Hill. Arquette eased into the landing circle. He still had 55 gallons of gas left, so he pulled out twice to make way for planes behind him that might be desperate for a deck. The third time he came around, the Bunker Hill turned off her lights. He made two more circles, waiting for the lights to come on again, then wandered off, looking for another carrier. A destroyer's searchlight pointed one out. He landed at 9:30.

The first thing he wanted was food, but when they took him to the wardroom, he discovered that he couldn't eat. He drank a Coca-Cola and four cups of coffee and smoked a half a package of cigarettes. What's the difference? I'm not going to get to sleep tonight anyway...

15

When Vraciu first saw the searchlights, his mind refused to accept their significance. It's Yap, or some other Jap island, or probably the Jap fleet. He picked up his microphone: "Gimlet Base from Gimlet Two-three, Gimlet Two-Three. Does our base have searchlights on?" The Lexington answered, "Affirmative. Land on nearest base." A glimpse of an Essex-class carrier had more significance than the lights. He moved into its landing circle, took a wave-off, and did not bother to go around again. He found another carrier and brought his plane aboard on his first pass. As he was taxiing up the deck, a plane ploughed into the barrier behind him. Vraciu heard it but did not turn his head to look. A crewman jumped on his wing after he had parked.

"What ship is this?" Vraciu asked.

"You're on the Enterprise, sir."

Vraciu did not listen to his answer. What difference does it make what ship I'm on? Why did I ask him? Around him, men were inquiring what repairs his plane needed, asking if he wanted coffee, admiring the eighteen Japanese flags on his cockpit, giving him directions to the wardroom. Their voices could not penetrate the thickening layers of his inertia and indifference. The first thing that he consciously heard was, "Some of your bombing squadron are on board."

He stumbled down to the bombers' ready room and shook hands twice around, slapping backs and having his own back slapped. He thought, Is it only four hours since we took off? We're acting like a bunch of brothers seeing one another for the first time in years! Brock would have enjoyed this...

16

The five TBMs crossed the screen together and circled, trying to find the Lexington. Norm Sterrie went down to 500 feet, with the other four planes strung out behind him: Bronn, Swanson, Cushman, and Thomas. The searchlights and starshells were dazzling. Planes from other air groups were charging through their column blindly, forcing them to pull up or swerve. Sterrie felt sweat running between his shoulder blades. He climbed back to 1000 feet, out of the melee, and steadied off. Bronn and Cushman closed in behind him. Swanson and Thomas were gone.

Presently there seemed fewer planes below. Sterrie dropped down again, searching for the Lexington's glow light. He found it, made his circuit, came into the groove, and the signal officer brought him aboard. He was waiting for his tail hook to be freed and the signal to taxi forward when an easy, unhurried voice came through his earphones: "Hello, Norm. This is Buzz. I'm going in the water."

McLellan shot down, Thomas in the water, three planes still to hear from. He looked at his wrist-watch: 9:30. The next ten minutes will tell the story...

He taxied forward and climbed out of his cockpit stiffly. Webb and Klingbeil were already on the deck.

"Well, boys," he said. "I got you home again."

They did not answer. They may not have heard him; the five-hour roar of the engine still echoed in their ears, and the fresh memory of the gamut above the force still occupied their minds. It was the first night landing either of them had made.

Sterrie dragged himself along the catwalk. When he stumbled into the lighted ready room, blinking, the other pilots and the intelligence officer surged around him and clapped his back.

"Hey, boy, welcome home!"

"How'd it go, Norm?"

"Get a hit?"

He couldn't answer: McLellan gone, Thomas gone, maybe more... He hung up his gear and dropped into a chair, haggard and unsmiling. Someone put a paper cup of brandy and pineapple juice into his hand.

Almost the first coherent sentence he spoke was ten minutes later, when Cushman came into the room.

Sterrie stared at him and said slowly, with a full accent on each word, "I'm damn glad to see you."

17

Cushman was making his second pass at the Lexington when he heard "Hello, Norm. This is Buzz. I'm going in the water." He was a pilot too experienced to let his thoughts linger on Thomas while his own plane was in the air. He coasted up the groove and let the signal officer wave him in. As he was taxiing forward, he got the brake signal. He was astonished at the mental and physical effort it took to respond, to press down with his toes. For the first time he realized how tense and tired he was. He took a last look at his gas gauge: just over 15 gallons, enough for about five minutes more.

The ready room welcomed him as it had welcomed Ster-rie: "How was it, Cush? What did you do?"

"Friends," he said, "I'll tell you: that stuff is only for the jay-birds!"

He reached for a cup of brandy and pineapple juice and drank it at a gulp. "God, that's wonderful!... How about Tom and Clint — any word from them?... Well, they'll be along in awhile. Hey, here's somebody now!"

The ready room door had opened, but it wasn't Bronn or Swanson. It was Dr. Baxter, bringing in the pilot of the SB2C that had crashed on the deck. Baxter's khaki shirt was streaked with sweat and smeared with blood. The pilot's shirt was torn across the shoulders, and the tear was blood-stained.

Baxter pointed to it. "Shrapnel," he said. "This kid's had a rugged time. I want him to tell you about it. Sit down, son... It'll do you good to get it off your chest, and it'll help pass the time for these other boys. See you later. I've got to make my rounds."

The SB2C pilot looked like a man in a nightmare. He kept his eyes on his shoes. When he finally spoke, the words came in a spate, but so low that they could hardly be heard.

"We caught a hell of a burst of flak over the fleet, incendiary stuff — thermite, I guess it was. It ripped this hell of a hole in my port wing, and the edges turned red hot and started to eat away. I kept watching it melt. I was hit in the back, here. I didn't know how bad it was, but I 'could feel the blood running down my back. This hole in the wing got larger and larger — all this happened pretty fast — and she fell off on that side and we started to spin. I pulled her out, but I found I didn't have any control under 110 knots. I figured we'd go in at any minute and I'd better make a water landing right there before the whole wing was eaten away, but pretty soon I saw the edges weren't red any more, so I decided to try to make it home. I watched that wing as much as I did the instruments. We got back, but I don't know how. I found this carrier, but the landing circle was jammed. I didn't have but a handful of gas left and no lights. I couldn't have made it around again. I knew I couldn't. I pushed my way into the circle. I saw the wave-off, but I couldn't make myself take it, I just couldn't... I wish to God I had, now. I'd give anything — Those men I killed—"

He got up and walked out.

Sterrie looked at the clock on the bulkhead: 10:15. If Bronn and Swanson had not landed on a carrier by now, they were in the water.

17

Swanson made two passes at one of the big carriers — he couldn't tell which — and was about to land when a plane cut inside of him so suddenly that he had to pull out to starboard. The loom of the carrier's huge island blotted the sky as he brushed past it. His gas gauge reported 15 gallons. He called Smith and LeBlanc on the intercom and told them, "Get set for a water landing!"

Just then he spotted another carrier, with a landing circle that seemed empty. The signal officer mistook the TBM for an SB2C coming in too low and made furious rowing motions with his paddles. Swanson had already straightened his lucky ring. He settled down to the best landing he'd ever made in his life. The carrier was the Princeton. His was the first plane aboard.

They took him to the officer of the deck, but all he could say was, "Take care of my crew, please." He repeated it, in a daze, "Take care of my crew…"

Another officer led him away and helped him get to bed. Presently the officer came back. "We're going to gas and arm your plane tonight. Will you be ready to fly in the morning?"

Swanson couldn't believe what he was hearing. "No!" he cried. "No! Not me!"

He turned his face to the pillow. It was next morning before his nerves let him sleep for half an hour.

18

When Tom Bronn located the Lexington, it was blacked out with a foul deck. His gas was low, and he considered pulling away to find another carrier, but decided to gamble on the lights coming back on in time. After two swings around the landing circle, he had gas enough for only one more. He made it. The Lexington was still blacked out, and the needle of his fuel-gauge was on "E."

He had already heard Thomas say, "Hello, Norm—" Now he felt like adding, "Hello, Buzz. This is Tom. I'm joining you."

He flicked the arm-master-switch twice.

Linson asked, "Prepare for a water landing — right?"

Bronn rocked his wings: "Affirmative."

"How long?" Linson asked. "Hick the light for the number of minutes."

Bronn flicked it three times.

"Three minutes — right?"

Bronn rocked his wings again.

Banazak could see the reflection of the lights in his plexiglas turret. He took off his parachute harness, and unlocked the escape hatch. Linson climbed into the middle cockpit. Each of them braced himself and waited for the shock.

Just ahead and to port, Bronn spied a destroyer. He curved toward it, blinking his running lights to attract attention, and let the plane settle. His exhaust flames gleamed back from the water, brighter and brighter. The plane hit and crushed to a stop.

19

Buzz Thomas lost the Lexington at the same time that he lost the other four TBMs. When he located it again, the landing circle was full, so he crossed over to the Enterprise, about 1000 yards to starboard. There he found room in the circle, but when he was on his downwind leg, he suddenly saw that he was flying head-on into six or eight planes on the upwind leg of the Lexington's circle. He ducked out, steadied off, and tried the Lexington's circle again. Still no room.

Stanfill asked, "How we doing?"

Thomas told him, "We've got between thirty and thirty-five gallons. When we get down to twenty, I'll give you the word to stand by for a water landing." Thirty gallons was enough for two, possibly three, more passes.

The landing circle stayed crowded. Thomas held away, watching his gauge. Twenty-five gallons, twenty...

"All right. Stand by! And Clasby—"

"Sir?"

"Get into the center cockpit."

"Aye-aye, sir."

Still no room in the circle. The needle went down: ten gallons, seven, five...

"We're going in."

"Roger."

"Roger."

As Tom Bronn did, Buzz Thomas picked out a pair of truck lights and flew close aboard, blinking his lights. It was a destroyer, he saw as he passed. A hundred yards ahead of it and fifty yards to starboard, he set the torpedo plane down. It hit once, bounced, and hit again, heavily.

20

Meanwhile, the SBDs were coming in. Weymouth took them across the screen and down in an S-turn. He had brought them home, and now his responsibility was finished. Every pilot would have to take care of himself from here to the groove. The last step was the longest. Even Weymouth had not made a night landing in over a year. Jack Wright had never made one.

Both the Lexington and the Enterprise had sent out warnings that their decks were foul with crashed planes, but two light carriers announced that theirs were clear. Weymouth broke off his section, Cook and Sedell, and went to find one. The undisciplined pattern of the lights confused him. What he thought was a carrier turned out to be two destroyers, one picking up the crew of a ditched plane, the other about to. Before he could orient himself, he had flown straight through the task force, and out into the empty darkness. Returning, he told McElhiney, "If you see a carrier, let me know."

Just then he spotted one, broke into the landing circle, and went aboard. It was the Lexington. As soon as his plane was chocked, he stumbled up the dark ladders to report to Admiral Mitscher. Flag plot's door was wired to cut off all lights when it was opened. Weymouth stepped into the black room and closed the door behind him. When the lights flashed on, the whole staff stood up [91] to welcome him, but the sudden glare made him blink, and there was a moment before he could distinguish the Admiral.

"God damn it, sir," he blurted, "we can fly at night, but we've got to practise like hell!"

He told his story and sketched out the disposition of the Japanese fleet, then went to air control, where he repeated it for Captain Ernest Litch, commanding the Lexington, and Commander Ernest Snowden, commanding the air group. Two of his pilots were in the bombers' ready room when he appeared, gray and drawn. At first, Weymouth did not seem to know where he was or who they were. Finally he said, "I'm sorry, fellows. I guess it was a pretty rotten job. I guess I lost Jay. I guess—" His voice trailed off.

21

Tom Sedell stayed out of the crowded circle for awhile. He had half an hour's gas left, so he could afford to give other pilots the chance that some of them needed worse than he did. When he had cruised for twenty minutes, the Lexington's circle thinned, and he came in.

His gunner, Maggio, had nothing to say. His best friend had been LeMay, Shields' gunner — the others called them "Hans und Fritz." He walked around the ready room shaking his head as if he were sick.

22

Orv Cook lost Weymouth and Sedell when they began to circle the Lexington. The first time he himself saw it was when he narrowly missed flying into its bow. He circled again and picked up the Enterprise. Two planes were ahead of him. The first was waved off, then the second, then Cook. The deck was foul. There was no way he could tell when it would clear, and his gas was running low.

He cruised in search of a light carrier but he couldn't find one. Presently he spotted another of the big carriers and slipped into its landing circle. By now he had ten gallons left, or enough for two passes. On his first pass, he got a wave-off. Next time around, he had just turned into his cross-leg when he saw a plane ahead of him, in the groove. If it was slow getting aboard and taxiing forward, Cook would be waved off again, and this wave-off would mean "good-bye!" Suddenly the groove was empty. The other plane was gone. No lights showed, no splash marked its plunge. It had simply vanished.

Cook hardly realized that he had landed until a plane captain appeared beside his cockpit. "What ship are we on?" Cook asked.

"Enterprise, sir."

He and Pop LeMieux said nothing. They shook hands and started down to the ready room.

23

Half an hour before Dupe Dupree crossed the screen, he told Dowdell to ask his wingmen, Glacken and Reichel, how their fuel stood. Dowdell hand-tapped the question and reported that each had forty gallons, which was less than half what Dupree himself had left. Dowdell was wrong. Each had ninety gallons. In hand-tap Morse, the number 4 is four fists, one palm, whereas 9 is four palms, one fist. In the darkness and the tension, someone made a mistake, but Dupree did not know it. He broke off his section, and stood aside in the security of nearly fifty gallons, hoping that Glacken's and Reichel's last few drops could squeeze them in to safety.

Don Reichel was turning into the Enterprise's groove when Landaker saw a fighter charging them from 8

"Pull up!" he yelled.

Reichel barely bobbed the nose of his plane, and Landaker froze to his seat until the fighter had flashed beneath them. Reichel explained calmly, "I didn't want to be cut out."

Landaker thought, Better to be cut out than cut up!

As they came into the groove, three planes splashed near them, one after another. Ahead of them was a fourth plane, too close ahead. Reichel knew he would get a wave-off, and that he couldn't make it around again. One moment he was following the fourth plane's lights, the next he saw them below him, burning in the water. Another moment, and Landaker was thinking, This is the greatest dam sensation in my whole dam life! Their tail-hook had caught a wire.

Reichel waited for the hook to be disengaged. He was hauling it back when he heard a crewman scream, "Brakes!" He jammed them on and looked around. His plane had been rolling backward. Three feet more, and it would have gone off the stern.

As they walked down to the ready room, Landaker never said a word, but he patted Reichel's shoulder all the way.

24

Glacken saw a searchlight shoot up from a carrier. He turned toward it, and suddenly the searchlight was coming from overhead. The vertigo passed as quickly as it had struck. He righted his plane and glided down, looking for the flight deck. Almost at the same time, he saw two things: his altimeter registered minus 10 feet, and the "carrier" was a destroyer. He yanked back the stick and was heading toward the screen when a flash of lightning revealed a light carrier dead ahead.

Boulanger, his gunner, saw it too. "That's only a jeep," he protested.

"What do you mean, 'only a jeep'?" Glacken said angrily. "We're going down!"

Just then the jeep blacked out. It made Glacken think of a drugstore that had turned off its lights one night, just as he put his hand on the door-knob. He made two passes all the same. Once the signal officer gave him a roger, but waved him off immediately afterward. Guess they've got a full deck-load...

He picked up another carrier and took three more wave-offs. He didn't have to look at his fuel-gauge to know what it was warning him: gas enough for one more pass, two at the most. He came up the groove again — it was the Lexington, he could see now — and got a fourth wave-off.

He called Boulanger: "Last time around!"

Boulanger said, "Roger!"

The signal officer straightened Glacken in the groove, raised him a little, and brought him in. When his tail-hook caught, he whooped at the top of his voice. He had three minutes' of gas in his last tank.

25

Cookie Cleland broke off Irish Caffey and Jack Wright and took them down. Slipstreams from stray planes tipped Cleland's wings and tossed him about, knocking him off-balance and off-course. He felt as if his brain were drying out, turning to dust. He made mistakes in judgment, knowing that he was making them. He tried two landings on the Princeton, two on the Lexington, one on a destroyer, and two on the Enterprise. He had no recollection of finally landing aboard the Enterprise. He didn't come to his senses until he was taxiing up the deck, and his engine died. He wanted to jump out right there and pat Old 39's cowling. She did it with her last gasp, God bless her!

A deck handling crew shoved him the rest of the way to the bow, shouting at one another to look at the jagged hole under Hisler's cockpit, the long rip in the starboard flap, the 20-miUimeter hole under the starboard tank. They were all distraught. A few minutes before, something had happened which no one had believed possible. The signal officer was waving in a fighter when an SBD without lights dropped almost on top of it. The men in the catwalks ducked. The firemen grabbed their extinguishers and rushed in. There was no crash, no explosion. The fighter's tail-hook caught the second cable; the SBD's, the fifth. Both planes came to smooth stops, unharmed.

The deck crews were still nervous from their escape. A plane captain dashed up and tried to pull Cleland and Hisler out of their seats. "Get out!" he yelled. "Step on it! We've got to push this damn thing overboard!"

Cleland remembered the attack on Palau. Old 39 had been crippled there, too, and he'd landed on the Enterprise then, too, and then, too, they had wanted to push her over the side. He had talked them out of it, and he started talking now.

"Can't help it," the plane captain said. "The old crate is busted to hell, and we haven't got room for her. Get clear!"

Cleland reached for his pistol. "God damn you," he said, "that plane stays aboard!"

The plane captain said, "OK, sir. If that's the way you feel about it...

26

Jack Wright, who had never made a night landing in his life, spotted a big carrier, found a gap in the circle around it, and settled lightly to the deck. They told him he was on the Enterprise.

"My God," he said, "the same old bucket I left a few hours ago!" But it seemed like weeks ago.

27

Irish Caffey lost Cleland and Wright soon after the break-off. The Lexington was blacked out, he saw, but a light carrier was near by. Well ahead of Caffey in the landing circle was a TBF from the Bunker Hill. Cookie Cle-land's SBD had used its last drop of gas as it was taxiing up the Enterprise's deck, but this TBF eked out an even narrower margin of fuel. Its engine died just before it crossed the ramp, and the pilot had to coast in with a dead stick. His hook caught, but the wire snapped the plane down hard enough to break its landing gear, and the signal officer was waving off all other planes until a deck crew could push the wreckage over the side.

Caffey took three wave-offs, then called Estrada: "Not much gas left! We may have to ditch." On the fourth time around, they got another wave-off, and Caffey told him, "We'll pull up alongside and drop it in."

Estrada had never made a water landing but he knew what to do. He slipped out of his chute, collected his gear, held his flashlight and waited. The plane hit. The instant it stopped, Estrada jumped over the side, all set to haul out the raft — and found a deck crew staring at him in astonishment.

He dropped his gear and remarked, "This water landing business isn't as bad as I thought it'd be."

He and Caffey always got out on opposite sides. Caffey came around the tail and saw Estrada's gear.

"I'm sorry," he said. "I saw a chance to sweat us in, and I forgot to tell you."

Light carriers are too small to accommodate any plane whose wings can't be folded, so the crews weren't used to SBDs, which have rigid wings. One of the crewmen started yelling at Caffey, "Fold them wings!"

"This is an SBD," he explained.

"God damn it, fold 'em anyway!"

Caffey and Estrada were too tired to go into it. They didn't want to talk to anyone, even to the men who had them by the arms and were guiding them to the ready room. There they each drank a brandy and water, between questions: "Did you get a hit?" and "Much AA?" and "How was it out there?"

Caffey answered the last question. "Once in a lifetime is enough."

28

Bill Linn was on the same carrier. He had landed his crippled TBM there immediately after his take-off from the Lexington, He saw Caffey come aboard, then turned to watch the next plane in the groove. Something in its vague silhouette was different, wrong. At the same moment, the signal officer saw something else wrong: the tail-hook was not extended. He threw a flashlight beam on it to warn the pilot. The beam lit up the fuselage, and a large red circle. The plane was a Jill, one of the newest Japanese torpedo planes.

The signal officer snatched up his wands and waved them over his head. The plane veered away, toward the Lexington, where it was given another frantic wave-off. Then it appeared close by the Bunker Hill, which shouted its alarm over the air: "All planes on this frequency get clear of our landing circle! There's an enemy plane in our landing circle, and we're going to open fire!" Before it could fire, the Jill was gone, ranging toward another carrier. Every ship in the task force snapped off its lights. Gun crews were ordered to be ready. The night's hysteria was now complete.

The Japanese pilot may have been lost, and as desperate for a deck as any American pilot in the air that night. His obedience to the wave-offs suggests it. But no one dared assume that he came in peace, and now no one will ever know. A cruiser caught him with its searchlight and saw him lurch and stagger and spin into the sea.

29

Dupe Dupree was still circling when he heard the Bunker Hill's warning. His gas was now down to twenty gallons. He found the Lexington and made three passes, but each time he was cut out by planes driving up from astern and crowding in ahead of him. He was too busy to get worried about a water landing. He had to dodge the wild planes and still keep one eye on the ship and the other on his instruments. The Lexington's circle did not thin out, so he pulled away for a pass at the Enterprise. Just as he took his place in line, there was a deck crash, and all the lights were turned off. By now his fuel gauge was registering empty, but he had clocked his consumption and was fairly confident that he had enough gas left for one more pass, perhaps two.

He called Dowdell. "It don't look like we're going to get aboard here. You want to bail out?"

"Me bail out? Strictly no!"

"OK. We'll keep punching. But make sure your guns are secure and your belt's tight."

Dupree began to check his own crash equipment. He screwed down the four valves on his life jacket, remembering the time off Pearl Harbor when he had parachuted into the water and found that one of his valves was loose. His shoulder straps were equipped with a spring that would yield when the plane struck, yet would keep him from being thrown forward and fracturing his skull. He took hold of the instrument panel and pulled against the spring, testing it. It broke.

He called Dowdell and told him about it. Dowdell dreaded a water landing almost as much as he dreaded bailing out. He said, "I believe we can make it, Dupe."

"OK, but it's going to be mighty close."

He flew back to the Lexington and tried another pass. His interval was large enough, but the plane that landed ahead of him did not taxi up the deck, and he was waved away. Dupree knew that his fuel gauge might be wrong, but his watch wasn't. Hell, he thought, I've been a gentleman long enough! He made a tight turn and cut back into the groove. It was all clear.

John Shuff picked him up with his wands, and Dupree had less than 200 feet to go when his engine died, out of gas.

When Dowdell realized what had happened, he swung his revolving seat dead aft, where it locked into place, and braced himself, eyes closed, waiting for the impact. Dupree let the plane drift down until it was ten feet above the water, then stalled it, to kill its speed, and snapped his stick so that the starboard wing-tip would hit first and throw him into the side of the cockpit, instead of into the instrument panel. An instant before they hit, he dropped the controls and grabbed the panel with both hands.

God damn! he thought. God damn it to hell, I could have held in the palm of my hand enough gas to get us aboard!

When the wing-tip hit, it slowed the plane. Then the wheels hit, and it tripped, turned a somersault, and crashed in on its back. The open cockpits acted as scoops.

The plane sank at once.

30

Shuff had not heard Dupree's engine quit. He signaled him "too low!" and "too slow!" all the way down to the water. After the splash, he turned to Hanson: "There's another guy we could have gotten in. Christ, what an awful night!"

Extracts from the Lexington's logs for the hour since the SB2C crashed on her deck show a part of what had happened around her:

"2124. Plane ditched on port beam.

"2134. From a destroyer: One in the water off our starboard quarter. Do you see him?

"2136. Plane ditched on port beam.

"2144. From a destroyer: We are going to pick up plane that crashed on our starboard beam.

"2146. TBF in water on port beam.

"2154. From a battleship: We hear a cry for help on our port quarter.

"2157. Plane in water on starboard beam.

"2158. From a carrier: A plane just went in the water about 500 yards astern of us.

"2159. From a destroyer: I am in line to pick up that man.

"2214. From a cruiser to a destroyer: Pick up a man on my port quarter."

Shuff had given up hope of landing planes smoothly. All he wanted was to get them aboard, right side up, and if they were within falling distance of the deck when they crossed the ramp, he cut them down. He dived into his safety-net five times. Once he jumped into the gun mount beside him and waved a low plane in from there. After awhile, Hanson took over the wands. He had to pry them loose from Shuff's stiff fingers.

31

When the bombers made their S-tum after crossing the screen, Harrison lost the three sections ahead of him. He and his wingmen, Moyers and Adams, spiraled down on their own, and presently Pinky Adams saw him give the break-off signal and swing wide to the left. Adams let him take his interval, then broke off in turn, close to the lights of a carrier that he believed was the Lexington. He circled once, but as he was making his final turn into the groove, he saw that the carrier's lights were far left of where he had expected them, so he made a hard left turn. He was astonished to see that the signal officer's wands were almost on the deck, indicating that his plane was dangerously low. As Adams gave it the gun, he glanced at his wing. *//1 reach out, I can scoop up a glass of water!*

He climbed, kicked right rudder, and skidded into the groove. He knew that he had to straighten his plane fast, because he couldn't take a wave-off; he didn't have enough gas for another circuit. The signal officer gave him a roger, a "fast," and then a cut. Adams hit the deck wheels first and bounced twenty feet into the air. *My God, I'm going to land in the Admiral's lap!* But he had caught a wire.

He did not notice that it snapped him down hard enough to spring his landing gear. He was numb with relief — so numb that the plane handler's signals had no meaning for him. *Why is this guy shining those lights in my face? What does he want? Oh, pull up my tail hook! Why didn't he say so?... Now what? I remember: that means 'Taxi forward.'* He took his toes off the left brake, stamped on the right brake, and taxied straight toward the island. He knew he was going to hit it, but the consequences meant nothing. *OK, we're going to crash into the island. So what?* A red light impacted on his consciousness just in time.

Kelly did not wait for Adams to park his plane. They were still taxiing forward when he climbed out on the starboard wing and threw his arms around Adams' neck.

"Pinky," he said fervently, "I love you! I love you!"

A plane handler saw him and yelled, "Get off that wing!" He jumped up in Kelly's place and told Adams, "You're on the Enterprise, sir. Do you need a guide to get to the bomber ready room?"

Adams was incredulous. "The what? You're sure?" He looked around and recognized the Enterprise's unique stack.

"Damn if it isn't!" he said.

His was the first SBD aboard. In the ready room, they gave him a stiff brandy, but he couldn't finish it. He handed it back. "I've got a belly-full of war," he said, "and no room in it for drinks."

32

Harry Harrison was the next one into the Enterprise's ready room. He had found a carrier, lost it, and found another, and was on his downwind leg in the landing circle when a destroyer suddenly loomed ahead of him. He didn't miss its foremast by five feet. If he had hit it, what would have happened to him and Ray Barrett never occurred to him; his only thought was for the men on deck: *Poor bastards, they must have figured I was going to smack 'em for sure!*

He curved into the groove, and the signal officer picked him up. He was making a V of some sort, but his wands were so nearly parallel that Harrison couldn't tell whether or not the V was inverted. It seemed not to be, meaning that he was too high, so he glided down, waiting for a roger. All at once he saw that he was below the ramp, looking up at the wands. He hauled back his stick and was still climbing when he crossed the ramp. The signal officer gave him a "fast" and a quick "cut." Harrison pushed over, but held it too long. He bounced, and when he knew that he had missed the wires, he pushed over again.

It felt like the smoothest landing he had ever made. Actually, it was a barrier-crash. His undercarriage buckled, and the propeller gouged into the deck, wrenching the engine to a stop. The plane was ruined.

A moment before, Harrison's spirits had been resilient enough to absorb a jolting crash. Now that he saw that he had fouled the Enterprise's deck, his exuberance vanished. *Twenty guys will go in the drink while they're clearing away this mess, all on account of me! Fifty guys, maybe!... I'm a murderer, that's what, and their ghosts will haunt me the rest of my life!*

He didn't wait to see the crew throw his plane over the side. He ran down to the ready room and bolted a brandy. It was two days before he could sit still for five consecutive minutes.

33

Don Reichel came into the ready room next, then Jack Wright, then Cookie Cleland, the squadron's "eager beaver." When Pinky Adams saw Cleland, he pushed him into a corner and demanded, "Cookie, have you had enough?"

"Well, it was pretty grim out there," Cleland told him.

"That isn't what I asked you. Have you had enough?"

"It was pretty hot, all right."

Adams persisted, "That still isn't what I asked you. Have you had enough?"

Cleland said soberly, "Yes, Pinky. I've had enough."

Adams was making Cleland repeat his admission for the rest of the squadron when Orv Cook and his gunner came in. Pop LeMieux's age was a standing joke with the pilots and other gunners. After every mission, they always asked him, "How about it, Pop? Still young enough for your job?" And LeMieux always answered, "Me? Sure I'm young enough! Sure I am!"

They asked him the routine question now. His answer was slower than usual. "No," he said. "I'm forty-three. I guess I'm too old to fly…"

34

Hank Moyers lost Harrison, his section leader, and Pinky Adams, the other wingman, when they broke off to make their first pass at the Lexington. He oriented himself and was on the cross-leg of his approach when a strange plane shot directly in front of him, so close aboard that its slipstream knocked him down until he expected his wheels to trip on a wave crest. He pulled up and started around again. This time he had no trouble. He landed on the Lexington with seven gallons of gasoline, the first SBD to make it aboard.

When they reached the ready room, his gunner, Lee Van Etten, threw his camera into a chair. "Take the God damn thing!" he cried. "I'll never use it again! I'll never fly again! Never!"

One or two of the more uproarious bomber pilots had sometimes wondered if the quiet Moyers was "rugged" enough for their squadron. Van Etten ran over to him and grabbed his shoulder and sobbed, "Hank, you're it! You're plenty rugged enough for me! You're the rugged-est damn pilot in the whole rugged outfit!"

35

The last two SBDs in the formation were Kirkpatrick's and Conklin's. They found a carrier and passed it on its starboard side. Conklin caught a glimpse of an Essex-class silhouette and told himself happily, That's her! That's the Lex, our little home from home!

Kirkpatrick circled once, shook his wings, and broke off. He had gas to spare and could have stayed up for a while, but the circle was empty, so he came aboard. When the tail-hook caught, his earphones seemed to explode. It was Bentley, yelling "Yippee!" Kirkpatrick smiled and rubbed his stomach: Good old safety-belt! Good old tug in the guts it gives you!

In the ready room, he saw that the other pilots were staring at him queerly. He didn't understand until they told him that his forehead was bleeding. He knew that he had kept his seat high and shoulder straps loose so that he could watch for stray planes, and he had probably lurched forward into the instrument panel when he landed. He didn't remember.

The squadron intelligence officer asked for his story. Kirkpatrick said, "Well, I've been jumped worse by Zekes, and there've been missions when I've had to be on the ball more, and I've landed with less gas, but I've never had all that trouble together until now. It was the Hop Supreme.

"As for the AA, I've seen it at Midway and Santa Cruz, but I'd never seen it like that from the top. Thank God, there's one big difference between the Japs' AA and ours: ours hits."

36

Conklin was all ready to follow Kirkpatrick aboard, when the Lexington turned off its lights. He circled again, but the truck lights of a destroyer confused him, so he pulled up to 500 feet and started another approach. He was almost in the groove when a stray plane shot up from the wrong side and would have crashed into his canopy if he had not ducked until the water threw back the red glow of his port wing light. He jerked the stick and started his third approach. Just then someone called, loud, "Prepare for a water landing!"

Sample asked anxiously, "Is that you?"

"Nope, it wasn't me," Conklin told him. "We're going to make it."

Another stray tried to cut him out, but the signal officer gave Conklin the wave-in. Sample did not know what carrier they had landed on until they were taxiing forward, and he saw the Japanese flags stenciled on the Lexington's bridge, marking the planes her AA had shot down. Conklin had hardly cut his switches before Sample was leaning into his cockpit, beating him on the back.

Together they headed for the island and the ready room. Inside the island, three men were lying on the deck. Sample pointed to them. "Funny place for guys to be caulked off this time of night!"

A radioman heard him. "Two of those guys are dead," he said.

They were the men who had been killed in the crash of the SB2C.

37

Dr. Baxter continued his rounds of the ready rooms, checking them for signs of over-stretched nerves. Occasionally he led a man off to sick-bay, or sent him to bed with a sleeping-pill, or simply gave him a regulation 1.6-ounce bottle of medicinal brandy. He offered one to a young torpedo pilot from another air group, who was huddled with his hands pressed under his arm-pits to conceal their trembling.

"No, thanks," the pilot said. "But what wouldn't I give for a glass of fresh milk!"

As the brandy took hold, taut nerves began to relax, and as they relaxed, the men began to talk. They told their stories over and over, to other pilots and gunners, to yeomen, to the mess attendants in the wardroom, to anyone who would listen. Baxter encouraged them. He knew how it reassured them to hear the sound of their own voices, after those long hours of silence in the air. He told them all, impartially, "You did a magnificent job! Magnificent! It's all over now. You'll never have to go through it again. But you did a magnificent job while it lasted!"

A fighter pilot took him aside. "Something I want to tell you in strict confidence," he said. "Know the only reason I got back? I'm going to get married when I get home, and I knew I couldn't unless I got back."

"That's natural!" Baxter told him. "That makes sense!" He patted the pilot's shoulder.

38

The Lexington landed twenty-two planes that night, but only ten of them were hers. Fourteen more were reported on other ships. Three more were known to have been shot down. Wendorf, Bronn, Thomas, Dupree and their crews were missing.

39

Cold water spurting through the shattered canopy of his cockpit shocked Wendorf into consciousness. His Hellcat had come to rest on its back, and he was hanging head downward in his shoulder straps and safety belt. He ripped open the buckles with one hand, using the other to prop himself from falling. The crash had slammed the canopy shut and mashed its rails. He had to work his fingers into a crack and pry it loose. As it yielded, such a cataract swept over him that he realized for the first time that the plane was under water.

He took a last breath, braced his feet against the seat, and shoved. Just then the canopy slid down again, fouling his parachute and raft, and pinioning his back. The plane was sinking fast enough for him to feel its pressure. His lungs were afire; oil slimed his nose and mouth; there were knives against his ear-drums. He budged the canopy and kicked again. He was free of the plane, but its suction was slow to relax. He drifted to the surface limply. A minute passed before he could think to trip one of the toggles that inflated his life-jacket, another minute before he was strong enough to trip the other. Then he lay back, gasping.

Pilots always remove their parachute harness before landing on a carrier, but Wendorf's sudden crash caught him unprepared. When he had rested, he struggled out of it and unlatched the raft from the chute, which started to sink. Too late it occurred to him that his back pack, containing his flashlight and Verey pistol, was still fastened to it. He managed to hook the harness with his foot, but the weight of the chute dragged his mouth under water, and he had to let it go.

Ordinarily, it requires only a minute or two to break the raft from its cover and inflate it. In his weakness, Wendorf needed nearly an hour, and the effort left him too exhausted to climb in. He could only tuck his elbows over the gunwale and hang there, waiting for his strength to build up. While he waited, a heavy cruiser passed within a hundred yards, close enough for him to distinguish the dim outline of her tripod foremast. He shouted, but his voice was no more than a faint, choking rasp.

A man must have the wind at his back when he climbs into a rubber raft, or it will be blown over on top of him. Wendorf could not locate the wind, and the raft blew over. He righted it, rested, and tried again. It blew over again. He squirmed aboard on his third try, but the raft swamped, and he rolled out. It had taken him some twenty minutes. On his fourth try he made it.

One of his shoes had been torn off when he escaped from the plane. He bailed with the other until he found the sea-anchor, and presently the raft rode high. The lifejacket would do for a pillow. He was folding it into shape when a spasm of nausea nearly shook him overboard. The oil and water he had swallowed were churning in his stomach, strangling him. He wiped his eyes and fought down another spasm just as a far-off destroyer's searchlight wheeled past him, briefly silhouetting something afloat nearby. Another pilot in the drink? He cleared his throat and shouted, "Hey, there! Hey!", but no one answered.

The vague object drifted closer. It's a piece of wreckage from my plane, that's what! Soon it was close enough to touch. He was about to reach for it when he saw that it was moving. It was a shark. Another followed it, and another.

Wendorf became a madman. He pounded the water with his shoe, then threw it at them, screaming and cursing. The fins glided off, but turned and came back until they were three feet away. His screaming made him retch again, and his retching made the raft tilt. He was terrified that it would upset, or that the sharks would puncture it and sink it. He thought of his pistol. The next thing that moved, he shot at. He fired eight times before nausea overwhelmed him again, and when the spasm passed, the sharks had disappeared.

A destroyer with a searchlight cruised by within possible earshot. He shouted, but they did not hear him, and it seemed that every time the beam swept over him, his raft slid down into a trough. If I'd only been able to keep that back-pack, with my flashlight and Verey shells!...

Another destroyer cruised by. Now that the sharks were gone, he ventured to paddle the raft around to face the searchlight. His hand touched something: a line. He hauled it in and found the raft-cover, with a first-aid kit and a tin can. Fresh water, thank God! His throat was raw. He had started to break the seal when he thought, Hold on! Somewhere or other, I've seen liquid dye-marker in a can exactly this size. Suppose I swallowed some in the dark, and it was poison... He strained his eyes to read the label. If only I had that flashlight! He stowed the can in the raft and waited for dawn.

His terror had gone with the sharks, and now even his worries began to fade. They'll search this whole area in the morning — bound to. It's just a matter of sweating out the night. He curled up and tried to sleep, but just as he sank into a doze, a searchlight flared toward him, and he jerked back into wakefulness. He tried to read the label again. Still too dark. Never mind: it'll be dawn soon.

Dawn was six hours away...

40

Tom Bronn and his crew were clear of their TBM in seconds. Banazak, the last one out, reached into the life raft hatch from the port side, but Linson already had the raft on the starboard wing, with Bronn. Banazak climbed over the cockpit to help them inflate it. The night was so black, they couldn't tell whether or not it was right side up. They were fumbling with it when Bronn called, "Inflate your life jackets, and let's get off this thing. It's going down! And watch out you don't get caught in the tail!"

They slid off the wing, dragging the raft. It was upside down.

By now the destroyer was near them. Bronn waved his flashlight and blew his whistle until a voice called, "Hold on! We'll be back!"

Linson watched the truck lights dwindle and vanish. "I wish I was home in Brooklyn," he said.

They were still struggling to right the raft, twenty minutes later, when Bronn saw truck lights again. Again he waved his flashlight and blew his whistle, and Linson and Banazak yelled. A searchlight leaped out, felt around for them, and held them while the ship coasted up. They could see its bow; it was a cruiser.

Somebody on deck called, "Hey, is it wet out there?"

They answered together, "Hell, yes!"

Bronn felt happy now. He called, "How's the chow on board?" He didn't listen to the answer. His whole attention was focused on his happiness.

A motor whaleboat splashed down and hauled them over the side. "What's the name of this ship?" Bronn asked.

"Reno. Where are you from?"

Presently they were in sick bay, sluicing off the salt water. Linson found it had ruined his picture of his wife, but one of the corpsmen turned out to be from Brooklyn too, so there were other things to talk about. Banazak took it all in his stride. A week before, he had lost his luck-piece, the little plastic Scottie, so he had expected a foul-up of some sort: getting off with a dunking was cheap enough.

Tom Bronn couldn't sleep. The day rolled and re-rolled in front of his mind's eye: I should have tried landing on another carrier... Wonder where

Mac and Hutch and Greenhalgh are right now?... I might have made it to another carrier... How about Buzz?... How about Mac?...

Several times in the night he got up for a drink of water, but as soon as he was back in bed, it started again: Buzzie... Another carrier, even a jeep... Mac,... Paul Dana, Newby Landon, Bob Isely, all killed in the past week... Now Buzz and Mac...

41

Stanfill hauled the raft out of Thomas' plane and spread it on the port wing. Thomas and Clasby had climbed out to starboard, and Thomas was trying to salvage as much of his flight gear as possible — his back pack, shells for his Verey pistol, his parachute. He tossed them out on the wing and looked at the heap, deliberating. Suddenly he said, "The hell with 'em!" and climbed over the cockpit to the raft, with Clasby. The three men pushed it off the wing and stepped in.

The destroyer they had signaled seemed about to stop near them when a Verey star burst somewhere off to starboard, and it dashed in that direction. Thomas and Clasby flashed their lights, blew their whistles and fired their .38s, but the destroyer kept going. Stanfill's escape hatch had been submerged when he climbed out, and the water he had swallowed made him sick. He vomited and fell back in the raft.

In a quarter of an hour, the destroyer was back. It was the Gatling. The pilot they had gone to pick up was from another torpedo squadron. Later, in the wardroom, he told Thomas about their day. Three of their five torpedoes hit, he said, but his division leader had been shot down. The plane had flamed and rolled on its back and plunged in with the whole crew.

"It was rugged seeing them go. They were swell guys…"

41

As soon as Dupree's SBD came to rest, upside down, he undid his safety belt, kicked free from the cockpit and swam under water until he was clear of the starboard wing. Only the plane's tail was still above the surface. If the water had been smooth, he might have been able to reach the life raft in the fuselage hatch, but the wake tumbled him about helplessly. He had ditched close aboard the Lexington, dead astern, and her four huge propellers were shoving her along at 22 knots.

Above the splash and froth, he heard Dowdell scream, "Dupe! Dupe!"

"Are you hurt?" Dupree called.

"No, I'm O.K., but come over here!"

Dowdell's scream was so frantic, Dupree called again, "What's the matter? Are you hurt?"

"No, but come here!"

The sinking plane was between them. As Dupree started to swim around it, the tail towered like a whale's flukes and slid under. Dowdell clutched Dupree's shoulders, pinioning his arms, but Dupree broke away, then swam back cautiously and gave Dowdell his right wrist to hold. Dowdell'6 life jacket had bulged out in front of him and was bobbing his head under water. Dupree shoved the jacket down and helped him crawl on top of it, but Dowdell was too weak to stay there. Every time he vomited, his head rolled under again. He had come up beneath the wing twice and had swallowed water; now the rough wake was making him swallow more.

As the ship moved away, the wake subsided to a slick, and Dupree was able to take stock. What he needed most was a raft, but the raft had sunk with the plane. What he needed next was a flashlight, for signaling, but that had sunk too; he had dropped it in the cockpit when his engine sputtered and had never been able to find it again. A pistol would have helped — its flash could be seen a long way at night — but he had no pistol, either; two days before, his parachute had been re-rigged, and the new straps were too tight to buckle over his shoulder holster; he had had to leave it off that afternoon.

Dowdell never carried a flashlight and he had lost his pistol. A flare gun was stowed in his cockpit, but he'd had no time to salvage it. The only signal equipment they had left was two dye-markers apiece. Dupree knew that they were devised for daylight use, but he had a desperate hope that the powder might also have a phosphorescent quality. With four of them, he could afford to risk one on the chance. He pulled the tab and searched the water around him for even the faintest glow. There was none. The only lights he could see were searchlights from two destroyers, one in the screen several miles to port, the other several miles astern.

The more Dupree thought about his predicament, the blacker it seemed. The task force was steaming East to land its planes, but soon — perhaps in a few minutes — it would reverse course to renew pursuit of the Japanese fleet.

He had no way to signal as the ships went past, and once they were past, they were past forever.

He shook his wrist. "They'll get us all right, Dan."

Dowdell did not answer.

Presently Dupree said, "Dan—"

"Yeah?"

"Can you pray?"

Dowdell said weakly, "Can I pray? All this time I've been praying!"

At that instant Dupree saw it — a black object riding up on a crest between himself and one of the destroyers. It sank into a trough, but when it rose again, not ten feet away, he could distinguish it plainly: a life raft, all inflated.

There was a moment before he could speak. He gestured toward it with his free hand. "Let's go get it."

"You get it," Dowdell said.

Dupree tried to tow him, but had to shake off his grip. He took three strokes, brought the raft back, and climbed over one end while Dowdell rested on the other. Dowdell had trouble getting in. His life-jacket caught, and he fell back. Finally, he hooked one foot over the rim and Dupree pulled him aboard. He landed backwards. For a while he refused to turn around, for fear the raft would upset.

As they settled down, Dupree saw that an emergency kit was dangling alongside. He hoped it contained flares, but it was empty. The disappointment hardly dented his new confidence. They could float for days now, and a search-plane would find them sooner or later.

Then came their second stroke of luck: Dowdell found his .38. The holster had swung behind him when he struggled free of the sinking plane, and he had thought that it was lost. He shook the water out, loaded one round, and when a wave hoisted the raft, he aimed toward the light of a destroyer astern, hoping someone on deck would spot the flash. The pistol only clicked.

Dupree said, "Ammunition's wet. Too bad."

Dowdell opened the cylinder and felt the cartridge. The firing pin had hit an empty chamber. This time the pistol fired. They waited, but the destroyer made no acknowledgment.

"Never mind," Dupree said. "Look yonder!"

A plane was heading directly toward them, led by a searchlight from the destroyer to port, low on the water, to show the pilot his altitude. They fired the .38 again, almost down the beam, but it swept on by. The plane — they could tell it was a TBF — passed close overhead. They followed its lights, watching them sink lower and lower. Soon the nose of the engine stopped abruptly. Another plane circled above them losing altitude. Soon, its engine stopped too.

Dupree said, "We've got a lot of company in the water tonight."

They threw away their shoes, to save the thin rubber raft from a puncture, and settled down again, resigned to waiting for dawn. At intervals, Dowdell vomited. Twice the raft upset. They had climbed back the second time when Dupree saw a destroyer silhouetted against a far-off light. It was less than a mile away, on a course that would pass them close aboard. When it was 500 yards away, Dowdell fired two shots. Just then Dupree spied a second destroyer, much nearer. Dowdell fired toward its bridge, and a searchlight flashed on, hunting the sea. Both men screamed and splashed water in the air, hoping it would sparkle. The beam swung toward them, caught them and held them.

"Boy!" Dowdell said.

The destroyer threw them a line and drew them alongside to a rope net. When they stood on the deck, Dupree said, "Looks like they can't kill us, Dan. God must be saving us for something big."

They considered bringing the raft aboard — "It ought to be preserved in the Smithsonian," Dupree said — but they decided somebody else might need it and happen on it as they had.

The medical officer took them below and examined them. Except for a few scratches, they were not injured. After they had washed away the salt, the doctor asked if they would like some coffee.

"No, thanks," Dupree said.

"Water?"

"No thanks."

"How about a brandy then?"

"Okay," said Dupree.

The destroyer — it was the Terry — had already picked up two other pilots that night. One was Comdr. "Killer" Kane of Air Group 10, from the Enterprise. This was his second rescue within a few days. His F6F had been shot down near Saipan, but he had been retrieved in time for the attack on the fleet. Coming back, he was in the landing-circle, making a time-turn on instruments at what he thought was a safe altitude when salt spray splashed into his cockpit, and his plane ploughed under.

The other pilot was from the Bunker Hill's torpedo squadron. The Terry had picked him up and his gunner, but his radio operator had gone down in the plane.

42

Wendorf's raft rocked through the night. He vomited once more, but finally his stomach settled. It would be dawn soon, and he could read whether he had a can of fresh water or a can of dye. Dawn had not yet come when a light carrier suddenly loomed near him. He opened his mouth, but all words fled from his mind. "Ahoy!" he finally yelled. "Ahoy, you!"

The officer of the deck heard him. His voice roared over the bullhorn, "A pilot on the port side! Drop a smoke light over!" Then, to Wendorf, "Pilot, there! They'll pick you up in about fifteen minutes!"

In five minutes the destroyer C. K. Bronson was throwing him a line and towing his raft alongside. It was 4:15 when he climbed aboard. As he peeled off his wet clothes, he discovered that his back-pack, with the flashlight and Verey pistol, had been strapped to his shoulders the whole time. But the little tin can was gone. He still wanted to learn whether it contained water or dye.

43

Before darkness fell completely, McLellan had hopes of finding a piece of flotsam buoyant enough to support him — a crate from the sunken carrier, or a few deck planks. Now that it was black night, he substituted the hope of attracting someone's attention, anyone's.

He unzipped his back pack and felt around until he located his Verey pistol and its six flare-cartridges. He fired a red star, waited two minutes, fired his .38, waited ten seconds, and fired his .38 again. He timed the intervals with his wristwatch. It wasn't supposed to be waterproof, but it still ticked along. Between shots, he waved his flashlight and blew his whistle and shouted.

He had considered the possibility of a Japanese ship answering his signal, and had decided that it meant only a probable death, against a certain death from exposure or drowning. He was already convinced that he hadn't the slightest chance of rescue. Once he thought of putting his pistol to his head and getting it over with right then, but he told himself in disgust, Hell, I'm no Jap! No hara-kiri for me!

The decision lifted his spirits. He had kept his waterlogged shoes for the remote event that he would get ashore, somehow, and need them. Now he scuffed them off, adjusted his life-jacket more comfortably, and began to sing. No Love, No Nothin' was his favorite song. He sang it over and over, until the salt water swelled his tongue and shriveled his lips, and made his voice a senseless mumble.

A few hundred yards away, Hutchinson was singing too. He ran through some current tunes, then hit on I'm an Old Cowhand. The more he sang it, the better he liked it. Here he was riding along on the waves, up and down, up and down, just like on a horse. He sang it again, louder.

Hutchinson never heard McLellan's pistol and never saw his flare, but Greenhalgh did. He took a bearing on the stars, fired three shots in answer, and started swimming. His line was upwind, and the sea exhausted him, but whenever he stopped to rest his numbing legs, waves washed over his head and made him choke. His canteen became unhooked and drifted away. It frightened him to lose it, but he had that much less to drag through the water. He patted himself to see if there was anything else he could discard: a pistol, a flashlight, two knives, a New Testament his father had carried in the last war. He might need every one of these, but his shoes could go. Untying them, he suddenly remembered that they were borrowed from Ike Davidson, a gunner in the squadron, and that Davidson had threatened to murder him if he lost them. The idea made him grin, feebly. Well, Ike, murder or not, here goes your shoes!

Davidson's threat made Greenhalgh think of his girl. When he wrote her about being shot down at Palau, she had answered, "Be careful, Selbie, and don't you take any more chances!" There's another laugh! He started swimming again, but he passed McLellan in the darkness. The waves seemed to be running higher. He began to pray.

Toward midnight McLellan fired another star and two more shots. Lights flashed back, blinker lights. He tried to read the message, but presently he realized that it was from a Japanese destroyer to a plane circling overhead, evidently looking for survivors. Greenhalgh saw the blinker too and waved his flashlight, but neither the plane nor the ship made any response. They patrolled the area for an hour and a half before disappearing in the northwest.

By now McLellan's tongue had swollen to such a size that he could hardly find room to move it. He opened his canteen to rinse the salt from his mouth and took one swallow. Immediately he vomited, then again, and again.

He tried to lean back in his jacket and rest, but water trickled into his ears. If he faced the waves, they splashed up his nose. It was useless to turn his back; he always drifted around again. Every two hours, throughout the night, he vomited. It seemed to take exactly that long for him to swallow enough salt water to bring on an attack.

Somewhere — he couldn't remember the place — he had read the line, "There are no atheists in fox-holes." It needed a postscript, he decided: And none in Mae Wests, either. He said his prayers over and over, but bits of nonsense kept intruding on his mind: *We could pass the time nicely if another guy came along and we had an acey-deucy set that would float and we could see the board...* He wasn't frightened. He had become wholly fatalistic. *If my number is up, it's up, that's all. If it isn't, it isn't. Either way, there's nothing I can do about it.*

Hutchinson managed to doze through part of the night. He had been a fatalist ever since he joined the Navy. *A man's a damn fool to go to war* with any other philosophy. Only one thing worried him: If I could just let Mother know what has happened, so she won't go on hoping...

Greenhalgh had accepted the inevitability of death. He thought about the squadron going home without him, when their tour of duty ended, and wished he could be there to help them celebrate. *That radioman who bought the set of blues from me won't have to pay the $30 now.* Friends who had been killed in recent actions began to hover around him. One, a gunner who had been shot down at Guam, came close enough for Greenhalgh to tell him, *Stand by a while! It won't be long! And we can both start bitching about the chow again.*

A rain squall swept over the water just before dawn, and presently came the dawn itself, with a flight of cheerful, twittering birds. As the sun rose, several small black clouds stood out against the eastern horizon. To McLellan, one of them looked so absurdly like a French poodle, he felt like laughing. *Why wait for a rescue that probably isn't coming? Why not try, at least, to rescue yourself?*

The nearest land, Saipan, was 500-odd miles away, and his compass was useless, full of water, but he could take his directions from the sunrise and the steady trade wind. Confidently, despite his nausea and his swollen tongue, he swam toward the East.

Greenhalgh didn't see the poodle. To him, the clouds resembled letters of the alphabet, particularly three, which made a perfect I and T and C. A few minutes before he noticed them, he had found a pencil in his pocket, one that his minister had sent him, with a picture of Christ and the text, "I will not fail you." He had brooded over it, reflecting that his own faith had gone. Then he saw the clouds. I,T,C... I,T,C... *Why, it stands for "I Trust Christ!"* All at once he was flooded with a determination to survive.

A sharp whistle sounded, and more whistles, and two men's voices. They came from every side, even from above, until Greenhalgh thought that his mind was going astray. Planes, too, seemed to be nearby; he heard them clearly, but he could not trust his ears. At last he spied them, twenty or more, so high that he could barely identify them as SB2Cs with fighter escort. One of his dye-markers had already gone, burst by his fall. He prayed as he pulled the other.

McLellan stopped swimming and glanced at his watch when he heard the engines. It was 7:30. He had four packets of dye, but he knew the stain would be an almost invisible pinpoint to planes at such an altitude. How about the mirror, though? He ripped off the adhesive tape that fixed it to his jacket and tried to aim the flash, but the tossing waves jostled him out of hope, and the tiny planes droned on. No matter: they've got the right course, and others will be following them.

They followed in half an hour — eight F6Fs, only 500 feet off the water, on a heading that would bring them close by. McLellan jerked the tab from a dye-marker. The green perimeter had hardly begun to expand when the last fighter turned out of line. In a moment all eight were circling overhead. One dropped a life raft twenty yards away. McLellan was halfway to it when he saw it rise on a crest and slide down into a trough; he never saw it again. Five minutes later, another raft was dropped, but this one fell fifty yards away, and he had no strength even to start toward it.

Then the TBMs roared up — TBMs from his own squadron — and rafts rained down all over the sea. Each of the three men grabbed one and inflated it and struggled aboard. Each, from his new elevation, looked around him. Still none saw either of the others.

McLellan wanted only to lie back and forget the terrible night, but first he made himself put over the sea-anchor, to steady his drift. He rinsed his mouth from the canteen and was just relaxing when a violent attack of nausea seized and shook him. It was so much worse than the ones before, he thought he had been poisoned by swallowing some of the dye. He retched until his throat burned and his belly-muscles ached. The attack left him too weak to wash down the raft, but too dizzy to care. He pulled the sail over his body and wet it to keep the sun off and fell asleep. Hutchinson and Greenhalgh were already asleep.

44

Buzzie Thomas woke up when one of the Gatling's crew brought in his clothes, dried and pressed. The trousers looked unfamiliar.

"You sure these are mine?" he asked.

"They're the ones you had on, sir."

Thomas looked at them again. Stamped inside the waistband was "Wilson."

I get it... I get it... So that's why my good-luck charm — his wife's handkerchief sewn into his helmet — couldn't get me home; it was out-jinxed! These were his roommate's pants, and "Pappy" Wilson had been in the drink three times...

The Gatling put them aboard the Lexington at 2 o'clock that afternoon. Thomas went to find Wilson right away.

45

The Reno transferred Bronn and his crew to a destroyer, which delivered them home in a breeches buoy. As Bronn stepped onto the Lexington's hangar deck, he saw Norm Sterrie waiting.

"Was Mac picked up?" Bronn asked. "How about Buzz?"

Sterrie said, smiling, "We're all accounted for!"

46

Another attack of vomiting woke McLellan after he had slept for an hour. When his dizziness passed, he found that his fingers and lips were losing their stiffness, and that he could move his tongue. But now, for the first time, he felt a surge of panic: Where are the float-planes? Why don't they come? Maybe I'm beyond their range, or they've crashed or been shot down or the fleet's turned back. He searched the horizon. Nothing was there, not even a bird, and there was no sound except the slap of the waves against his raft. He slept again, restlessly, with cruel dreams.

Greenhalgh had fallen asleep without waiting to open the raft's emergency can of water, although he had had nothing to drink since he lost his canteen. Nor had he covered himself with the sail. When he awoke, he reached for the can, but he could not move his right arm at all. His flight suit had not been enough protection from the tropical sun, and his whole body throbbed. He managed to open the water-can, but when it was empty, he was thirstier than before. The first-aid kit held a few rolls of bandages. He swaddled his burning face and wrists and ankles, and poured water over them.

Weakness from vomiting had brought on McLellan's panic. The agony of sunburn brought on Greenhalgh's. Where are those planes? Are they going to leave me here to cook to death? He splashed more water on himself, to occupy his mind and lure it back to calmness. Hutchinson, a few hundred yards away, slid up and down the crests, humming and whistling, watching the East. His shadow overflowed the raft, and began to lengthen in front of him.

McLellan awoke at 4 p.m., with the unmistakable tone of F6Fs in his ears. He knew that they would be escorting float-planes and presently he saw them — four OS2Us, Kingfishers, laboring along behind. Three of them settled in the water some distance away. The fourth circled as if it did not intend to alight. McLellan had drawn his pistol — later he asked himself why — when the plane landed near him and taxied over, and the pilot leaning out, grinning. "How about it? Want a lift?"

McLellan croaked, "You're the best sight I've seen since I've been living!"

He crawled onto the pontoon, but couldn't climb up to the rear seat. The radioman had to help him in. They passed him a cupful of ice water, but he vomited it over the side. When he was able to talk again, the pilot asked his name and what he had seen, and transmitted it back to his ship, a cruiser.

They took off and circled until the other three planes joined them. In one McLellan saw hair of a familiar red. It was Hutchinson, smiling from ear to ear. He tried to ask him about Greenhalgh, but Hutch couldn't read his hand-taps. The pilot offered to query the other planes, but no word came back. McLellan gave it up; he was still too queasy to talk much. He swallowed hard until he fell into a doze, and slept most of the way back to the task force. As they crossed the screen, another OS2U flew alongside, and there was Greenhalgh, waving feebly. McLellan gave him an inquiring thumbs-up, but Greenhalgh turned his thumb down. His hands and face were burnt scarlet.

Greenhalgh's pilot had made two landings, the second one to pick up a gunner from a torpedo squadron. He told Greenhalgh that a Japanese had swum up to his raft that morning and had tried to climb aboard. The gunner kicked at him and started paddling away. He was unarmed, but the Jap wasn't. He swam after the raft for half an hour shooting at it whenever waves lifted them at the same time.

The ship's medical officer treated Greenhalgh's burns and gave McLellan a brandy and water, the first drink he was able to keep down. He had hoped to rest, but Admiral Mitscher wanted his report at once, so he and Greenhalgh were transferred to a destroyer and sent across to the Lexington. Hutchinson's plane was from another cruiser; he was returned separately.

Aboard the destroyer, McLellan tried his stomach on a large glass of pineapple juice. It didn't sit too firmly, so he asked one of the officers in the wardroom to show him the nearest toilet, as a precaution. When he found it was only ten steps away, he had enough confidence to heap his plate with scrambled eggs, toast, jelly, butter, and three scoops of strawberry ice cream. They all stayed down.

"I lost fifteen pounds last night," he announced, "but there's four of them back right there."

He and Greenhalgh were put aboard the Lexington at 8:05 p.m. and were taken to the flag bridge at once. Admiral Mitscher was in his usual seat, facing aft.

"Glad to have you back," he told them. "What did you see?" He listened to their story, then said quietly, "I think we might have got one of them."

Greenhalgh spent that night in sick-bay. His skin and nerves were so raw, Dr. Baxter gave him a pad and told him to write down everything he could remember about the attack.

His last page, the sixteenth, ended, "When we got aboard, the pilot told me he had just 10 gallons of gas left. These boys with the rescue planes do a wonderful job and I was very grateful. It was the second time I had been picked up by them. With men like that, I wouldn't mind being shot down in Tokyo Bay, 'cause if there were any way possible they'd come after us."

47

The other gunners in Bombing 16 had always kidded Dowdell about his "Li'l Abner" shoes, a huge pair of Army field shoes he had bought from a Sea-Bee at Maui. The first thing they noticed when he rejoined the Lexington was his neat black oxfords, a present from the Terry.

"Hey, look!" they shouted. "Look here! Get a load of fancy Dan!"

They kidded him and slapped his back and shoved him around for a while before they began to tell him, "Glad you're back, Dan," and to ask what he had done and seen.

Next door, in the pilots' ready room, Dupree was already telling them. He'd seen something on the Terry you wouldn't believe. The crew had this little black dog — his name was Midnight — that would point land when they were seventy-five miles off-shore! Everybody on board swore up and down it was God's gospel truth. Point it! Stick his nose right on the bearing and bark! And another thing he'd do —

They had to hear about Midnight before he got around to his own story. When he came to the part about Dowdell hanging onto his wrist, he said, "I can't understand that. It's not like Dan to get scared."

One of the other gunners said, "That was because he can't swim, Mr. Dupree. Dan can't swim a stroke."

"Can't swim? What about the time he went in the drink off Pearl? He didn't say a word about it then!"

"No, sir. He was afraid if you found out, you wouldn't want him as a gunner."

Dupree said slowly, "Well, I be God damn! The little bastard..." He turned and shouted, "Dowdell! Dan! You come here to me!" When Dowdell came in, Dupree grabbed his shoulders and shook them. "Know what I'm going to do? The minute we get to a shore station, I'm going to teach you to swim myself! But you keep right on flying in that old rear seat until we get there. OK, Dan?"

"OK, Mr. Dupree."

48

Every one of the fighters who landed at all had landed on a different carrier. Henry Kosciusko did not know whether his wing-man, Bill Seyfferle, was alive or dead until he took off for the Lexington the next morning and saw an F6F with the number 33. Seyfferle saw him at the same time. He shook his wings, and grinned, and wiped his forehead in relief. Alex Vraciu joined them, grinning too, and holding up his thumb. Then they strung out to go aboard: Kosciusko first, Seyfferle second, Vraciu last.

Kosciusko had just climbed out of his plane when he heard a blast from the Lexington's siren and saw Vraciu circling over a widening patch of foam. Seyfferle had spun in. The crash had burst the package of dye-marker on his jacket, because the foam gradually became tinged with bright green. But nothing else came up. That was all.

49

Directly or indirectly, the attack on June 19th cost Air Group 16 nine of the thirty-four planes it sent out, and four of the sixty-four men.

50

Two weeks later, Captain Litch summoned the sixty survivors to the wardroom and presented each of them with a citation for a medal. You, the reader of this account, are probably familiar with the ribbons that represent these medals. In case you did not know what the medals themselves represent you know now.

ROSTER

Roster of the officers and men of Air Group 16 who saw action in the attack on the Japanese Fleet, listed in the order of take-off:

FIGHTING 16

Lieutenant Henry Marzy Kosciusko, U.S.N.R.,
Live Oak, Fla.
Age 27. Married.
Awarded Gold Star in lieu of third Air Medal.
Previous awards: Air Medal and Gold Star.

Ensign William John Seyfferle, U.S.N.R.,
Cincinnati, O.
Age 22. Married.
Awarded Air Medal (posthumous).

Lieutenant (junior grade) Arthur Payne Whiteway, U.S.N.R.,
Haddonfield, N. J.
Age 23.
Awarded Gold Star in lieu of second Air Medal.
Previous award: Air Medal.

Lieutenant (junior grade) John Wilson Bartol, U.S.N.R.,
Port Washington, Wis.
Age 23.
Awarded Gold Star in lieu of third Air Medal.
Previous awards: Air Medal and Gold Star, Distinguished Flying Cross.

Lieutenant James Alvin Seybert, Jr., U.S.N.R.,
Ottumwa, Ia.
Age 26.
Awarded Gold Star in lieu of second Air Medal.
Previous award: Air Medal.

Ensign Edward George Wendorf, U.S.N.R.,
West, Tex.
Age 22.
Awarded Air Medal.
Previous awards: Distinguished Flying Cross and Purple Heart.

Ensign Homer Weston Brockmeyer, U.S.N.R.,
Earleville, la.
Age 21.
Awarded Distinguished Flying Cross (posthumous).

Lieutenant (junior grade) Alexander Vraciu, U.S.N.R.,
East Chicago, Ind.
Age 24.
Awarded Gold Star in lieu of second Air Medal.
Previous awards: Distinguished Flying Cross and Gold Star. Air Medal.

Lieutenant (junior grade) James Howard Arquette, U.S.N.R.,
Eagle, Idaho.
Age 23.
Awarded Gold Star in lieu of second Air Medal.
Previous award: Air Medal.

TORPEDO 16

Lieutenant (junior grade) Clyde LeRoy Bronn, U.S.N.R.,
Long Beach, Cal.
Age 22. Married.
Awarded Navy Cross.

Eugene Paul Linson, ARM1C, U.S.N.R.,
Brooklyn, N.Y.
Age 23. Married.
Awarded Distinguished Flying Cross.
Previous award: Air Medal.

Michael Aloysius Banazak, AOM 1C, U.S.N.R.,
Everson, Pa.
Age 22.

Awarded Distinguished Flying Cross.
Previous award: Air Medal.

Lieutenant (junior grade) Warren Ernest McLellan, U.S.N.R.,
Fort Smith, Ark.
Age 22.
Awarded Air Medal.

Selbie Greenhalgh, ARM2C, U.S. N.R.,
Pawtucket, R.I.,
Age 22.
Awarded Purple Heart and Gold Star in lieu of second Air Medal.
Previous award: Air Medal.

John Seaman Hutchinson, AMM 2C, U.S.N.R,
Burbank, Cal.
Age 21.
Awarded Air Medal.

Lieutenant Kent Manning Cushman, U.S.N.R.,
Tacoma, Wash.
Age 25. Married.
Awarded Distinguished Flying Cross.
Previous awards: Air Medal and Gold Star.

Francis Ora Frede, ARM1C, U.S. N.R.,
Los Angeles, Cal.
Age 30.
Awarded Distinguished Flying Cross.
Previous award: Air Medal.

Phillip Jackson Layne, AMM1C, U.S.N.R.,
Trenton, Mich.
Age 24.
Awarded Distinguished Flying Cross.

Lieutenant (junior grade) Clinton Vance Swanson, U.S.N.R.,
Minneapolis, Minn.

Age 25.
Awarded Navy Cross.

Rene Joseph LeBlanc, ARM2C, U.S.N.R,
Sanford, Me.
Age 28.
Awarded Distinguished Flying Cross.

William Holmes Smith, Jr., AMM 2C, U.S.N.R.,
San Antonio, Tex.
Age 19.
Awarded Distinguished Flying Cross.

Lieutenant (junior grade) Harry Charles Thomas, U.S.N.R.,
Chicago, Ill.
Age 28. Married.
Awarded Navy Cross.
Previous award: Air Medal.

Robert Gerard Clasby, ARM3C, U.S.N.R.,
Waltham, Mass.
Age 23.
Awarded Distinguished Flying Cross.
Previous award: Air Medal.

Grady Lester Stanfill, AMM1C, U.S.N.R.,
Fullerton, Cal.
Age 25.
Awarded Distinguished Flying Cross.
Previous award: Air Medal.

Lieutenant Norman Anderson Sterrie, U.S.N.R.,
St. James, Minn.
Age 26. Married.
Awarded Distinguished Flying Cross.
Previous awards: Navy Cross and Gold Star, Air Medal and Gold Star.

Howard J. Klingbeil, ARM 1C, U.S.N.,

South Bend, Ind.
Age 23. Married.
Awarded Distinguished Flying Cross.
Previous award: Air Medal.

Jack William Webb, AMM1C, U.S. N.R.,
Toledo, O.
Age 26.
Awarded Distinguished Flying Cross
Previous award: Air Medal

BOMBING 16

Lieutenant Commander Ralph Weymouth, U.S.N.,
Santa Barbara, Cal.
Age 27. Married.
Awarded Navy Cross
Previous awards: Distinguished Flying Cross and three Gold Stars, Air Medal and Gold Star, Presidential Unit Citation.

William Arthur McElhiney, ARM1C, U.S.N.,
Salem, Mass.
Age 21.
Awarded Distinguished Flying Cross Previous award: Air Medal.

Lieutenant (junior grade) James Albert Shields, U.S.N.R.,
Houston, Tex.
Age 22.
Awarded Navy Cross (posthumous)
Previous award: Air Medal.

Leo Ovila LeMay, ARM2C, UJ3. N.R.,
Worcester, Mass.
Age 23.
Awarded Distinguished Flying Cross (posthumous).
Previous award: Air Medal.

Lieutenant (junior grade) Thomas Roy Sedell, U.S.N.R.,
San Leandro, Cal.

Age 23. Married.
Awarded Navy Cross
Previous awards: Air Medal and two Gold Stars

Anthony Charles Maggio, ARM2C, U.S.N.R.,
Richmond Hill, N.Y.
Age 23.
Awarded Distinguished Flying Cross
Previous award: Air Medal

Lieutenant Thomas Earl Dupree, U.S.N.R.,
Gordon, Georgia
Age 24.
Awarded Navy Cross
Previous awards: Air Medal and Gold Star

Daniel David Dowdell, ARM2C, U.S.N.R.,
Jackson Heights, L.I.
Age 20
Awarded Distinguished Flying Cross
Previous award; Air Medal

Lieutenant (junior grade) George Thomas Glacken, U.S.N.R.,
Fort Wayne, Ind.
Age 27. Married.
Awarded Navy Cross
Previous award: Air Medal.

Leo Wilfred Boulanger, ARM2C, U.S.N.,
Fall River, Mass.
Age 20.
Awarded Distinguished Flying Cross
Previous award: Air Medal.

Ensign Orville Melvin Cook, U.S. N.R.,
Savanna, Ill.
Age 22.
Awarded Navy Cross

Theodore Henry LeMieux, ARM 2C, U.S.N.R,
Lawrence, Mass.
Age 43
Awarded Distinguished Flying Cross
Previous award: Air Medal.

Lieutenant Donald Kirkpatrick, Jr., U.S.N.R,
Evanston, Ill.
Age 27.
Awarded Navy Cross
Previous awards: Silver Star, Distinguished Flying Cross, Air Medal.

Richard LeRoy Bentley, AOM2C, U.S.N.,
Los Angeles, Cal.
Age 19.
Awarded Distinguished Flying Cross.
Previous award: Air Medal.

Lieutenant (junior grade) John Donald Reichel, U.S.N.R.,
Okmulgee, Okla.
Age 26.
Awarded Navy Cross
Previous award: Air Medal.

John Albert Landaker, Jr., ARM2C, UB.N.R.,
Cincinnati, O.
Age 21. Married
Awarded Distinguished Flying Cross
Previous awards: Air Medal and Gold Star

Ensign Eugene Vincent Conklin, U.S.N.R.,
Chanute, Kan.
Age 20.
Awarded Navy Cross
Previous award: Air Medal.

John Williams Sample, A0M3C, U.S.N.R.,

Delmar, Del.
Age 23.
Awarded Distinguished Flying Cross

Lieutenant William Edwin Harrison, U.S.N.R.,
Beverly Hills, Cal.
Age 23.
Awarded Navy Cross
Previous awards: Air Medal and Purple Heart.

Raymond Alfred Barrett, ARM2C, U.S.N.,
Springfield, Mass.
Age 19.
Awarded Distinguished Flying Cross
Previous award: Air Medal.

Lieutenant Cook Cleland, U.S.N.R.,
Cleveland, O.
Age 24. Married.
Awarded Navy Cross
Previous awards: Air Medal and two Gold Stars, Purple Heart

William Joseph Hisler, ARM2C, U.S.N.R.,
Philadelphia, Penn.
Age 23.
Awarded Distinguished Flying Cross
Previous awards: Air Medal and Gold Star

Ensign Henry Horace Moyers, U.S. N.R.,
Lilbourn, Mo.
Age 25.
Awarded Navy Cross

Robert Lee VanEtten, ARM2C,
Lakewood, New Jersey
Age 22. Married
Awarded Distinguished Flying Cross
Previous award: Air Medal.

Ensign John Franklin Caffey, U.S.N.R.,
Salt Lake City, Utah
Age 21
Awarded Navy Cross

Leo Dale Estrada, AOM2C, U.S. N.R.,
Maricopa, Cal.
Age 23.
Awarded Distinguished Flying Cross

Lieutenant (junior grade) William Lee Adams
West Palm Beach, Fla.
Age 25. Married
Awarded Navy Cross
Previous award: Air Medal.

Henry Francis Kelly, ARM2C, U.S.N.R.,
Troy, N.Y.
Age 23.
Awarded Gold Star in lieu of second Distinguished Flying Cross.
Previous award: Distinguished Flying Cross

Lieutenant (junior grade) Jack Lovell Wright, U.S.N.R,
St. Joseph, Mo.
Age 24.
Awarded Navy Cross.
Previous award: Air Medal.

Willard Newman Fellows, ARM2C, U.S.N.R.,
Watervliet, N.Y.
Age 20.
Awarded Distinguished Flying Cross
Previous award: Air Medal

The average age of the thirty pilots was 24; of the twenty-seven aircrewmen, 23. Eleven of the pilots and four of the crewmen were married.

A NOTE TO THE READER

WE HOPED YOU LOVED THIS BOOK. IF YOU DID, PLEASE LEAVE A REVIEW ON AMAZON TO LET EVERYONE ELSE KNOW WHAT YOU THOUGHT.

WE WOULD ALSO LIKE TO THANK OUR SPONSORS WWW.DIGITALHISTORYBOOKS.COM WHO MADE THE PUBLICATION OF THIS BOOK POSSIBLE.

WWW.DIGITALHISTORYBOOKS.COM PROVIDES A WEEKLY NEWSLETTER OF THE BEST DEALS IN HISTORY AND HISTORICAL FICTION.

SIGN UP TO THEIR NEWLSETTER TO FIND OUT MORE ABOUT THEIR LATEST DEALS.

Made in the USA
Coppell, TX
20 February 2020